Tactical LinkedIn® Secrets

ADVANCE PRAISE

"It is vitally important to have a strong network. David Cobb understands business networking and now has shared his knowledge in this powerful new book. The insights he shares in Tactical LinkedIn® Secrets *will help you build your networking game."*

–Pat Williams, Co-founder Orlando Magic,
Author of *Revolutionary Leadership*

"With so much change happening and priorities shifting, it's getting more difficult to stand out in an often-crowded marketplace. How do we do that? By making the right connections that create value add opportunities. David's book gives readers the most up to date tools they should develop to strategically connect with the right decision makers. It's not a popularity contest. Get this book if you want to elevate yourself from status quo connector to super connector."

–Jeffrey Hayzlett, Primetime TV & Podcast Host, Speaker,
Author and Part Time Cowboy

"Dave Cobb has done it again. He exemplified his "added value" mentality, not only in our firm's development, but through Tactical LinkedIn® Secrets, *to many strategic aspects of professional and personal development. Doing business with Dave is just good business. Make it your business to read his book. As with commercial real estate, his foray into authorship will not disappoint. It might just make your deal."*

–Ed Kobel, President & Chief Operating Officer,
DeBartolo Development

"*David Cobb's work speaks directly to the power of innovation driving business transformation today. As a fellow business leader, disrupter, and believer in digital empowerment to transform individuals, organizations, and communities—this book is one for your library. It serves a purpose in education at all levels, and is a profound enunciator of realizing how the digital world impacts every one of us.*"
—Raamel Mitchell, Microsoft, Central U.S. Corporate Citizenship and Market Development Director

"*Looks great! Very fun…love the Cobb Rants and all the references. It's easy and breezy, like the ultimate guide to LinkedIn®…excellent man.*"
—Irv Weinberg, Best-Selling Author and Muse/Mentor Extraordinaire

"*Just as ModWash and Hutton are defined by our unique culture, David Cobb creates a fresh book 'culture' with his digital immersion, and creative conveyance of technical info and practical tactics. As in his skill in commercial real estate, his prose is relentless, persistent, and materializes a provocative and lucrative deal. The tenets within are marketing musts.*"
—Karen Hutton, Owner and Founder of ModWash & Hutton Development

"*I know tackling, and Cobby has tackled delivering an exceptional book. As in our personal conversations, his writing addresses tactics, psychology, life, and his heart to help others. I'm deeply appreciative to him for exercising his skills on a new playing field, and often with my own kids. And he reconnected me to an old friend in a Fly way. Reading* Tactical LinkedIn® Secrets *is like watching game film with a top-notch coach.*"
—John Mobley, Former NFL Linebacker and 2X Superbowl Champion (Denver Broncos**)**

"*Cobb let it fly!* Tactical LinkedIn® Secrets *is a best tactical catch in business and branding, especially for those casting for White Marlin relationships, appreciating the swells, and knowing the bait and tackle of strategy. Superconnecting? Cobb's quivered arrows reconnected me with John Mobley (2X Superbowl Champ and childhood friend) who is now tackling high-profile tournaments with me — baiting fish and hooking whale-like connections in an insanely fun atmosphere! Fish around, readers. No guppies in Cobby's blue ocean.*"

–Fly Navarro, Author of *Best Catch 2020*,
CEO FlyZone Fishing (Legendary Angler**)**

"*I was thrilled to be called a superconnector in Dave Cobb's,* Tactical LinkedIn® Secrets. *The tools promoted, which I use, are a pulpit to garnering connections that elevate your business, brand, and are exceptional for promoting charities, and ideas. Must read!*"

–John Crossman, Author of *Career Killers/Career Builders: The Book Every Millennial Should Read*,
CEO Crossman Career Builders

"*This is the top 1% of the top 1%.* Tactical LinkedIn® Secrets *is for serious connectors only—who REALLY want to take it to the next level. It is applicable for X'ers to Boomers. It's edgy, futuristic, and a renaissance of LinkedIn® competency. In today's culture of infinite transition, Dave's book teaches how to stay agile and connected for "what's next?" The QR Codes make it digitally genius. The rants? Insightful, fun. Game changer!*"

–Greg Sausaman, CFE, Author, CEO of
Cream 4 You International, LLC

"David Cobb has talent that makes writing and teaching an art. His debut book will help people to round the bases of success, and in the process, this kid is giving it all to charity to help young athletes find their voices on and off their field of play. His grandad, "The Georgia Peach," would be proud. Dave's book is a winning catch."

–Steve Nicosia, World Series Championship Catcher, '79 Pirates

"For anyone who is in business in this day and age, Tactical LinkedIn® Secrets *is a must read. David Cobb is a seasoned commercial real estate professional and marketing expert who has deciphered what can be a maze of information into proven, manageable concepts and tactical steps that, if followed, are sure to result in success for your business on LinkedIn®. Highly recommended reading."*

–David Wolf, Founder and CEO, Audivita Studios

"David introduced me to the power of LinkedIn®. Period. As a young commercial real estate executor, my aim is to build more exposure and be on the forefront of my network to gather intel, build relationships and garner quick responses. People pick up the phone when they know you. Tactical LinkedIn® Secrets *serves as a provoking and intelligent guide to catapult your progression."*

–Marti Weinstein, Associate, Zell Commercial

"Dave has written a must-read guide for anyone interested in elevating their business utilizing LinkedIn®. Whether you are just getting started with social media or you consider yourself a pro, Dave provides an easy-to-follow guide full of useful and practical tips everyone can benefit from learning. Highly recommend."

–Stacey Mooney, CRE Matchmaker, Founder/CEO, Retail Live!

Tactical LinkedIn® Secrets

RANTINGS FROM A SUPERCONNECTOR

Dominate in an Age of Noise, Competition
and Attention Market Share

DAVID COBB

NEW YORK

LONDON • NASHVILLE • MELBOURNE • VANCOUVER

Tactical LinkedIn® Secrets

Dominate in an Age of Noise, Competition, and Attention Market Share (Rantings from a Superconnector)

© 2022 David Cobb

Published in New York, New York, by Morgan James Publishing in partnership with Difference Press. Morgan James is a trademark of Morgan James, LLC. www.MorganJamesPublishing.com

LinkedIn®, the LinkedIn® logo, the IN logo and InMail are registered trademarks or trademarks of LinkedIn® Corporation and its affiliates in the United States and/or other countries.

Proudly distributed by Ingram Publisher Services.

Morgan James BOGO™

A **FREE** ebook edition is available for you or a friend with the purchase of this print book.

[_____]

CLEARLY SIGN YOUR NAME ABOVE

Instructions to claim your free ebook edition:
1. Visit MorganJamesBOGO.com
2. Sign your name CLEARLY in the space above
3. Complete the form and submit a photo of this entire page
4. You or your friend can download the ebook to your preferred device

ISBN 9781631957765 paperback
ISBN 9781631957772 ebook
Library of Congress Control Number: 2021948725

Cover Design by:
Christopher Kirk
www.GFSstudio.com

Interior Design by:
Chris Treccani
www.3dogcreative.net

Morgan James is a proud partner of Habitat for Humanity Peninsula and Greater Williamsburg. Partners in building since 2006.

Get involved today! Visit MorganJamesPublishing.com/giving-back

- Cady, Sydney, Kelsey—I love and treasure you always—my biggest and proudest accomplishments.

- To my Dad, Charlie—You're the kindest man I've known. And loved. You and Peggy are amazingly amazing together.

- To my Aunt Peggy and Uncle John—The perfect balance of Cobb toughness and love—humble thankfulness and love.

- To the friends younger, kindred and athletic comradery. Those of us who bonded and my support pillars in various chapters. You know who you are and how much you mean to mean. Thanks for a listening and landing foundation. I love all of you and heartfully-endeared-aforementioned.

- Lastly, to the people of Royston, GA and the Ty's in heaven. I never met or only knew in infancy. I hope this book makes you proud.

"Don't come home a failure." —Ty Cobb

TACTICAL CONTENTS

LET'S RANT. FOR PROSPERITY AND POSTERITY

G reat to meet you. I'm David Cobb, Florida-based leader, learner and complex curiosity who loves to communicate and superconnect. And make a profit while playing the game well, tactically and relentlessly with a strategic goal of focused intent. That game goes something like a chess match—or any combative sport whose rules of engagement incarnate warfare in peace.

Archery, basketball, even spiderwebbery all employ offense, defense, aggression, strengths, weaknesses, strategies, triumph and defeat. *Tactical LinkedIn® Secrets: Rantings from a Superconnector* takes the fight to the LinkedIn® arena and arms you as a social media tactician. Invincibility lies in hope and inspiration, knowledge and power. So embrace your inner warrior as we charge into digital battle. Trophies and spoils await in this novel business novel. Immersive, experiential and digitally interactive, my book will pull you into the content through QR codes and your smartphone—your sharpest and most agile katana in the new theatre of competition.

> The new LinkedIn® theater of competition is enabling small and medium-sized organizations (or humans) not only to compete at a different level, but to outmaneuver and outperform larger, established, cumbersome organizations through nimble creativity. Size doesn't matter.

Just as this book is going to teach you to stand out and gain competitive dominance in your marketing place, it also aims to stand out in the category of books about mastering LinkedIn®. Through secrets—beyond the LinkedIn® landscape—and antic scenarios and replays, my intention with this book is to demonstrate and divulge what works, and along the way to entertain. You will receive real-world teachings, real time and really applicable.

You will also catch some rants from my experiences as a superconnector. So let's spin some stories and interweave some connections and ensnare some relationships. Step into the Cobbweb, silked and nocked with Cobbisms. And, of course, rants.

What's in it for you? Results from, and insights into, mastering a platform that simply works if you proceed tactically to tier your relationships upward.

The tactical secrets provided are demonstrated through case studies and quantifiable achievements, showcasing real-world organizations and people across industry sectors. Multiple and actionable.

My partners and I at Archon Commercial Advisors leverage LinkedIn® to grow and evolve our boutique commercial real estate firm based in Orlando. We planted seeds and will teach you harvesting secrets. As we harvest. Pull out your sickle and take in the seeds of opportunities.

We like to think of it as: "Either you are LinkedIn® or you will be LinkedOut."

My quest in writing *Tactical LinkedIn® Secrets* is to share my experiences and help you profit in various forms, from expanding strategic relationships and increasing capital returns, to building credibility and facilitating access to innovation and innovators… and much, much more.

I initiated my LinkedIn® journey as a presenter at a Site Source conference in San Diego.

Site Source is a network of boutique commercial real estate firms, the members of which I dub a rag-tag gang of dynamic, unique and rogue entrepreneurs about whom you will learn more in ensuing sections.

In preparing my remarks, I did my homework. I explored the attendees' LinkedIn® profiles and found many, despite being digitally savvy, were in an abysmal state of not utilizing a tool that could escalate their business as well as their professional profile. I took them to town by showing how many followers each had.

The room buzzed as 103 hypercompetitive personalities had their LinkedIn® prowess or lack thereof digitally and frontally revealed. Our three partners had more followers than the next 10 principals combined. They were unknowingly missing the mark.

I was concerned for my friends. My goal was to illustrate a threat, spark an epiphany and create a call to action. After the room of type-A, hyper-competitive extroverts settled down, I enthusiastically shared many tactical LinkedIn® secrets and specific data showcasing the value of LinkedIn®.

My phone and email began to light up post-conference with many asking for help. I continued to school them, and my calibrated lessons were resonating. My new friends and colleagues began engaging in their own creative strategic marketing initiatives. These results-driven outcomes led me to the curation of teachings and case studies you will now have access to in this series.

The advice and knowledge provided will prepare you with what we coin as "arrows for your digital quiver." For those without knowledge of archery, your quiver is an assemblage of tools for you to apply and optimize.

To an entrepreneur or those traversing the C-suite echelons or simply we who are choosing to develop a personal brand, *Tactical LinkedIn® Secrets* is a five-rung climb to the top of the LinkedIn® funnel. Knowing the capabilities of LinkedIn® maximizes your possibility of reaching the summit.

It's your time to advance relevant solutions you can implement today. *Tactical LinkedIn® Secrets* will teach you to avoid pitfalls, cobra pits, the venomous, and design a content creation plan. You will know how to connect with elite thought leaders and spar with those who can further your goal to collaborate, conduct business, land a job or teach.

Go forth and arm your quiver.

YOUR GUIDE TO COMPETITIVE DOMINANCE

BUILDING RELATIONSHIPS, STATUS & WEALTH

"Always Spar with Those Better Than You"
–Jose Figueroa (MMA Fighter)

Tactical *LinkedIn® Secrets* is your guide to digital adeptness through a maze of pixelated noise. And what does that mean? Digital = Differentiation = Dominance.

In this section, I teach the attributes, features and benefits of LinkedIn®. You will move through the B2B maze like the all-powerful queen, the most ruthlessly efficient chess piece on your competitive chessboard. And you will have a quiver of tools like Robin Hood at the end of this short discussion and those ensuing.

If you're like me, you will be the hound who relentlessly digs up every unturned digital stone and gives the fox your best chase. *Tactical LinkedIn® Secrets* is unapologetic in this approach, yet also makes it fun and creative as your personality and professional essence start to shine through on LinkedIn®.

TOPIC 1:

DIGITAL = DIFFERENTIATION = DOMINANCE

Let's Do This...

In an ever-changing world, are those who survive the toughest, the smartest or the biggest? I assert that those who survive and dominate are the ones who are armed with tactical secrets. In the case of LinkedIn®, where I am willing to bet the farm that you already have a profile, the secrets are hidden in plain sight. Can you see them? If not, you are about to get your vision corrected.

> **Cobb Rant:** A word of advice: Approach the digital waters cautiously, deliberately and tactically. Digital tides will sweep out inconsequential posts, self-promotion and bland content. So how can you be deliberate and tactical?

The best place to begin is with a peek inside success.

TACTICAL APPLICATION:
LINKEDIN®'S POWER ACROSS GENERATIONS

Mike, 50, and Marti, 26

Archon Commercial Advisors joined the 45-member network of boutique commercial real estate firms called Site Source. I knew Site Source's individual and company brands were in trouble. If they didn't pivot, their relevance would diminish. Our message to them was that LinkedIn® is a perpetually evolving competitive digital chessboard that will crown kings and topple rank brands.

Two of my Site Source friends, Mike Guggenheim in his 50s and Marti Weinstein in her 20s, went from content consumers to established content creators by implementing my tactical secrets. Mike and Marti launched brands that exuded expertise, professionalism and knowledge among their industry peers and respective cohorts. They developed their "quiver" and executed on it.

> Site Source is a network of boutique commercial real estate firms, the members of which I dub a rag-tag gang of dynamic, unique and rogue entrepreneurs about whom you will learn more in ensuing sections.

As early adopters-turned-champions of LinkedIn®, both offer tactical applications. We will profile Marti more in depth in coming pages. The quantifiable figures are fascinating. Mike and I started the "Guggenheim Experiment" and continue to track its progress regularly. Marti Weinstein is a digital *La Femme Nikita*. Read about their execution and results and you'll see what I mean.

TOPIC 2:

FIRST IMPRESSIONS

DILEMMA: Lack of Preparation for Online Success

Strategic planning is the key separation point between master content creators and passive non-contributing consumers. LinkedIn® is the new theater of high-level business-to-business competition where the next generation of winners will be crowned and the losers will be vanquished.

> **Cobb Rant:** In many cases, the losers will never know why they failed, and it will haunt them for the rest of their careers. You know the ones I am speaking about. Those who incessantly lament their "problems", but don't understand that most of their hardships are only symptoms of an underlying source rooted in their own fundamental dilemmas.

Let's explore the most common pitfalls digital creators experience when making the initial jump into developing their LinkedIn® brand.

First and foremost, the majority are not tactically prepared to set that all-important foundation, which directly leads to a host of problems.

The first secret: Keep it real!

Your remedy equals your qualifications, credentials and communications.

Silly Mistakes–Unwittingly Creating Negative First Impressions

Okay, how about a solution? Reframe…let's create positive impressions.

An unimaginative LinkedIn® profile can put you in a precarious scenario where you can be viewed as vanilla or lethargic. Even worse, in extreme situations, it can damage your reputation.

LinkedIn® is a first impression gateway where your credibility is established. A subpar, mediocre or slack profile in today's fast-paced business environment will mar your good name. However, not having a basic LinkedIn® profile is tantamount to using a fax machine or not having an email.

Absent or outdated profiles are "dinosaur identifiers". I use the word *dinosaur* in the sense of archaic and out of touch. It is not a reference to those who have circled the sun repeatedly over the past several decades, as there are 70-year-old techies and 25-year-old dinosaurs. However, ageism is an unfortunate trend that technology is briskly accelerating.

Back in the "good 'ole days," your standard telephone was the conduit for audible communication between two people. The new trend is that the smartphone or other screen device is the conduit for imagery-driven and multi-sensory interaction among multiple parties. Inevitably, skillsets of the future will involve interfacing with such extensions of the human brain.

This human interaction with technology does not judge, though how we interface with and capitalize on it most certainly does, regardless of age. So is it ageism or resistance to embrace new tech interfaces? I believe the latter is the foundational dilemma and the former is the symptom.

To expand on this logic, there is a new order of operation in the world. For example, look at the history of job or career-oriented communications:

➢ 1600 BC Smoke Signal: "Village under attack. Time to soldier up."

➢ 1440 Printing Press: "First mass social media."

➢ 1860 Pony Express: "There's gold in them thar hills."

➢ 1980 Phone Book: "Hello! I am a people person! Call me."

➢ 1990 Fax Machine: "Hey you... I'm a people per (paper jam) son."

➢ 2000 Website: "See me? I'm here for you on the World Wide Web."

➢ 2020 LinkedIn®: "Name, education, experience, location, relationships, recommendations, writings, videos, photos, endorsements and much more."

It is clear that the way we communicate has evolved. We have also established that a dynamic, digital first impression is essential in the 2020s.

> The greatest question you can ask yourself is, "Have I evolved?" Are you digitally showing up in the 2020s or as if you were living in 2000?

The greatest question you can ask yourself is: "Have I evolved?"

Are you digitally showing up in the 2020s or as if you were living in 2000?

Keeping Up with the Digital Joneses (or Be a Jetson)

Parading a 15-year-old picture, sporting a college logo or peacocking a common industry title is worse than cowering as a digital ghost. It's a "skeleton profile."

Ghosts are invisible, but skeleton pages will keep you in the crypt of digital isolation and irrelevance. Skeleton pages are an in-your-face representation that a person is not keeping up with their Digital Jones' competition. As a ghost you can plead ignorance. As a skeleton, even an ignorant one, you appear indifferent or, significantly worse, lazy. Digitally emaciated.

> **Cobb Rant:** Your typical corporate bio is sterile, mechanical and lame. It's typically a headshot of a person over 50 wearing a tie or jacket. Make your imagery engaging, elicit positivity and show you're passionate about your goals. But please, I beg of you, do not use a selfie, cropped group photo or headshot from a previous decade. Those are worse than a 1980s church directory photo or glamour shot.

No one cares where you went to school, what your title is or what accreditations you have. Digital consumers are looking for a human connection, not a logo-branded connection. Don't get me wrong, credentials matter. However, people (aka your future customers or relational upgrades) want to know and trust you. Your CV gets you started. You have to do the rest, and that's a matter of brand recognition and communication.

Clickbye or Click-Buy?

Will potential relationships buy what you're selling or clickbye (meaning bye-bye baby) your profile? What are you selling? Your Personal Digital Brand (PDB).

First, let us take a detour and go human beyond the confines of static technology. For the next generation of office workers, hygiene and grooming will be required when working from home. Like it or not, the first impression many if not most will form of you will be through pixels on a screen. Those first impressions will be cemented when people view your LinkedIn® profile.

> **Cobb Rant:** As an added bonus, for the first time in history you can still look professional wearing an untucked shirt or a tie and a blazer, and pair that with hot pink basketball shorts and green flip flops. Yes, we have evolved into talking heads on a screen.

Technology is accelerating trends at an unprecedented rate, and the office worker paradigm is tectonically shifting to an expanded home-based workforce. That means the congregation will come together more frequently on digital screens and mediums. Zoom, FaceTime, Skype and a plethora of other apps will be the path of least resistance to expedite these communication trends.

As I reflect on 2020, I am awed by COVID-19's role in accelerating the LinkedIn® intercommunication tsunami.

QUIVER TACTICS:
GO TO COMBAT—ARM YOURSELF FOR
THE FIRST IMPRESSION

Now it is time to take action. These are your first steps in avoiding the three-second clickbye, which is tantamount to a potential soulmate swiping left on a dating app. Once the forthcoming tactical secrets are implemented, you will control the narrative for anyone deep diving your profile. Read on to become tactically armed for clickbuy execution in your relational web — and to ensure that dynamic relationships swipe right.

LinkedIn® or LinkedOut

A LinkedIn® contender must create a dynamic first impression on their homepage at a thoroughbred level when the digital gate stalls drop.

> **Cobb Rant:** Do not fall victim to a three-second clickbye, which is the ultimate terrifying scenario. Can you imagine that the most phenomenal opportunity of your career swiped left and hopped on to the next competitor because you didn't impress them on their first click? A three-second impression could have made your dreams come true, but you missed out because you weren't prepared.

Amazing LinkedIn® opportunities invisibly visit regularly, but you'll succumb to missed opportunity syndrome because you just didn't care enough to optimize your profile. The only remnant of your three-second clickbye will be clandestine and fleeting profile views.

> **Cobb Rant:** That would suck.

QUIVER TACTIC:
UPDATE YOUR RÉSUMÉ AND PROFILE (ONGOING)

Do not let your digital or even paper résumé become stagnant. And although the past does not necessarily equate to your future, it is still there and accessible. Quarterly. Minimum, yearly.

Pay attention or others will.

TOPIC 3:

THE DEEP DIVE

Your Digital Legacy Matters

What is the natural genesis of how people are specifically found and vetted in online investigations? Answer: Investigators deep dive. Don't be spooked, but the proverbial "they" can find you. When found, best to show the best you, and the best of your biz, and that you're best-in-class. Digitally. Perpetually.

When a digital mad hatter like me performs a business-related deep dive, the LinkedIn® rabbit hole is routinely the first stop. There's no telling how deep, dark and lucrative the rabbit hole can be. Lace it.

However, deep dives need to be planned, calibrated and strategic. Own it, meaning ruthlessly invest time and effort to achieve results.

LinkedIn®'s default settings will notify anyone within LinkedIn® that you viewed their profile each time you view them. Push notification is one of the benefits of the LinkedIn® Premium service. This means every time you view a Premium friend, colleague or competitor, they know instantly that you have viewed them. If you are creeping, the queens of the chessboard are keeping track. I am.

> **Cobb Rant:** First you must ask yourself if you want others to know that you looked at their profile. This is a similar predicament to searching a dating app. Don't be phony, Tinderoni or Bumble your way through the online social labyrinth. Planless? Really? You must decide whether you want to appear interested to the other person or whether you prefer to approach them in stealth mode. Your tactical outcome hinges on the approach.

Stealth Privacy Mode

For clandestine intelligence research, you may not want the person you are qualifying, or in my case dissecting, to know that you are digging around their digital legacy. The LinkedIn® "who viewed your profile" feature is a dead giveaway that you are actively on the hunt.

Let's say you seek to remain anonymous and conduct your tactical research without raising flags of engagement. Simply change your settings to "privacy mode." Shazaam! Now your name and profile only appear to psychics. So you can track who's creeping your profile while you stay on the down low.

> "Oh, and don't worry about the little covert op, all right? I'll keep it on the lowdown." —**GREG FOCKER**, *MEET THE PARENTS*

Benefits of LinkedIn® Premium

Standard LinkedIn® doesn't display Interesting Views, and only reveals the last five people who searched you. Interesting

Views is a filter setting that notifies you when a company or person you follow looks at your profile, or when industry leaders and influencers are perusing your musings. A life-changing relationship may have shown interest, but you would never know because you didn't upgrade. The epitome of LinkedOut. Advice? Just get LinkedIn® Premium.

This must-have service lets you see when browsers viewed your profile and how many times it was viewed in the last 90 days. Plus, you can follow up with a direct message sent via InMail, a critical perk only available through LinkedIn® Premium. Remember, though, to first save all prospective leads and Interesting Views in Sales Navigator. Built for B2B sales pros, this LinkedIn® Premium account type enables on-platform prospecting, including a space to stash your notes on profiles, and sales spotlights that show when people change jobs, appear in the news or follow your company.

> Establish a following through LinkedIn® Premium and watch your empire trickle-grow by the hundreds, eventually gushing into the tens of thousands.

The biggest potential relationship in your life simply inputs your name into the search bar, hits enter and within seconds sees your entire history, profile and characteristics. LinkedIn® becomes your armor on the frontline, and you get to choose how you want to be exposed. You have all the power on this platform to manage not only your accurate history but also the opportunity to neutralize potential outside threats.

This leads us to a very serious warning: You must remember that the deep dive doesn't end at LinkedIn®. No matter what you post—publicly or privately—that content will remain in cyberspace forever.

Cobb Rant: So yes, to answer the question you are most likely pondering, you should start today with a deep dive on yourself. The obvious, and sometimes not so obvious, first step is to delete the spring break twerking competition, competitive beer pong videos and the time you ran around a giant rock naked on a college tradition dare of a boulder run. *You are correct. I have done one or all of these, but you will not find them in my digital legacy.*

My first challenge to you is to investigate your digital legacy. Deep dive and root out anything that could harm your reputation or first impression.

QUIVER IT–Just a Little Bit!

TACTICAL MODUS OPERANDI–PERPETUAL DIGITAL RESUME (YOUR PDR)

PDR–Reputation Hazard & Protective Hedge

Some of you are probably a little confused because you didn't know you had a perpetual digital résumé or PDR. Newsflash: You do, and your colleagues, clients, co-workers, competitors and future lucrative relationships are paying attention. Your PDR is vital to the health and wellness of your reputation online and real world. It can ultimately make or break you. Without hesitation.

Quiver-Reversal (Definition):

Quiver (obsolete) "The collective noun for cobras." Snakes lurk all around seeking to malign you online and offline based off your PDR. Tactical LinkedIn® Secrets are the anti-venom. What do you want your competitors to talk about at happy hours? You. And your digital presence. I don't know about you, but I would rather be dissed than forgotten. Snakes will hiss. Forget about them.

> **Cobb Rant:** If all of your digital actions are self-promotional or even worse, self-aggrandizing, your reputation and influence will take a significant negative hit and it could take years after making a course correction to restore your PDR. Years...

In some circumstances, especially in today's gladiatorial media and ruthlessly fake competitive environment, you can quickly find yourself caught up in a story where you are cast as the villain. That negative press and suspicion are then quickly measured against your PDR, and if you have failed to pay attention and neglected to prepare, you will have inadvertently confirmed the accusations or suspicions made against you. Yes, your PDR is that powerful. Hello, Othello. Shakespearean tragedies occur all the time online. Be true to thine own self.

For some not-so-dramatic circumstances, your personal PDR can get stuck within an organizational framework where no external parties will ever see you or your content. The upshot? You are inward facing with actions that only your connections see. You are not reaching out beyond your immediate pool to play in the bigger ocean.

This can often happen within large corporate structures where you are striving to be seen, acknowledged for your contribution and competing for promotions. Assail your PDR up the ladder. Exposure is vital to hedge your future, because one day you will most likely be confronted with a career change, whether it be forced or chosen. The lack of a personal PDR will be your undoing in the transitional period where you will be LinkedOut without a LinkedIn® lifeline.

> **Cobb Rant:** From this point on you can never say you were not warned. Anything you post that is petty, taboo or violates standards of decency is a potential chicken that will look for a roost in the next lunar cycle. Edgy, quasi-controversial and thought-provoking content is a crucial component of our digital community, as is vulnerability. Malevolent, disingenuous, narcissistic and shamelessly promotional posts will not age well. Posts can be deleted, but screenshots and videos from other devices will haunt your brand for digital eternity.

Conversely, playing in the bigger ocean with a positive PDR can be an exhilarating experience. If you recognize the accomplishments of your allies and competitors, share knowledge and show authenticity, your PDR will shimmer. You will be held in high esteem and your reputation will precede you, as your digital diary is timeless. Your positive, uplifting and educational content will flourish forever in cyberspace.

Intentional Digital (PDR) Footprints

Today, a digitally naive child can ascertain in seconds what would have taken a private investigator days, or possibly weeks, to dig up only a few decades ago. Nine simple keystrokes: D-A-V-I-D C-O-B-B is how long it took someone to go to my profile and see that I:

➢ Paid for a professional picture.

➢ Am not a slob, have an A+ cowlick and invested in a fake grill white as the pure driven snow.

> ➤ Publish articles on various topics—some controversial and edgy.
> ➤ Have a passion for sharing industry knowledge.
> ➤ Cultivated a quiver of high-quality connections.
> ➤ Received phenomenal endorsements from industry leaders, colleagues and clients.
> ➤ Am an aspiring author who is very grateful for my readers.

My digital footprint was intentional, not accidental. This investment has netted rewards, both personally and professionally, far exceeding anything I could have anticipated or otherwise achieved. The most valued rewards are the generous guidance and advice received from mentors, friends and partners. You too can possess this collective knowledge. The choice is yours. Remember that it's all about how you stack up against your competition.

Is the LinkedIn® magnifying glass going to burn you like a digital ant or create a positive impression for your next dream lifelong connection?

Tactical Execution–Your Diary Creates Influence & Relationships

The critical component of your digital diary is the section that shows your profile, circle of influence and key relationships. In a deep dive, their findings can impress, be a non-factor or compel a guilt-by-association response.

A savvy digital tactician can figure out the following.

Covetous intelligence no longer exists. There are no locked filing cabinets, proprietary customer lists or real trade secrets anymore. Anything non-proprietary is available to an organization or individual as well as to their competitors in the unlocked digital competitive arena.

LinkedIn® can give you the reins to timeless, global and competitively advantageous knowledge at your fingertips. Optimize your profile for maximum positive exposure and arm your personal digital brand with as many credibility arrows as possible. Share knowledge, insight and positive stories, and karma arrows will reciprocate.

We have discovered that the hardest part for most is pushing outside of a certain comfort zone and getting started with a tactical plan. This is one reason I am sharing the secrets and you now have the digital LinkedIn® quivers at your fingertips. However, good intentions are only intentions unless they are realized, which requires time and effort. No getting around it. Wishful thinking is the same. You must invest in your thinking, time and effort.

Diligence impels creativity.

QUIVER TACTIC:
TAKE INITIATIVE
You must now take consistent action several times a week to engage with your identified targets in multiple ways. Touch arrows are about relating to your bullseye relationship. How?

Think of this as nothing more than interacting with friends and commenting or liking their posts or sharing their content. Set an alarm for 30 minutes and get it done as if your career depends on it, because it does.

KEYS TO EXECUTION

Surge ongoing waves of solid content. The great news is that it doesn't matter very much if your previous content was awful, offensive or self-promotional. You need to flood LinkedIn® with relevant, applicable and compelling posts. Consistent content will wash away your previous digital blemishes or posts that were lame. Cloaking them like a cover-up tattoo of an ex's name.

Deploy a calibrated and diversified content creation schedule. Construct calendar reminders and stick to them. Cluster and commit to a process. Begin with 30 minutes per day and post two to three times per week. Ten minutes commenting, 10 minutes researching and 10 minutes posting.

TACTICAL APPLICATION:
LINCOLN-DOUGLAS NATIONAL DEBATE CHAMPION

Don't believe me? We will discuss our first concrete, quantifiable and real-world example with dynamo and ninja attorney Tara Tedrow.

Tara has a reputation that precedes her as an esteemed cannabis legal specialist and a chained dragon you unleash at a land-use development hearing. The first time we met in person was at a group business lunch and I immediately intuited that she was edgy, razor smart and satirically indignant. She was also the three-time Lincoln-Douglas National debate champion at Wake Forest. I knew she had to be our organization's real estate land use attorney.

Then Tara gave a phenomenally insightful cannabis talk.

I had recently augmented our social media effort to make a splash in digital marketing, and asked Tara if she would write an article on the intersection of cannabis and real estate. She said yes. My post above received over 8,000 views, 78 likes and 16 comments. Tara's short form article below inspired me to write a blog and touched off my hard slide into short form writing (and now this book).

Tara Tedrow on Cannabis

Then I wrote my first article and non-business-mandated piece. It's amazing to see how skills can improve under the right-writing tutelage. Quick, dirty, persistent, earned, much improved and agile writing:

A Week of Cannabis: Presenting a Controversial Topic on Social Media & My Final Thoughts:

Fast forward to the summer of 2019 and I couldn't wait to share my recent LinkedIn® discoveries with Tara, knowing her limitless potential on the platform. We got to talking about social media and Tara compared LinkedIn® to all the other social media sites of which she was not a fan.

Tara conceded that LinkedIn® held out far more promise for advancing her legal career. She didn't have LinkedIn® Premium. I promptly requisitioned her cellphone, took her credit card and immediately upgraded her to LinkedIn® Premium. Within a few weeks, Tara's following had shot up by 20 percent.

Want to see Tara's debutante ball as a soon-to-be LinkedIn® baller? Obviously, we were having a fun and insightful conversation. A simple and engaging pic does the trick every time. Boom went the dynamite and I honestly couldn't believe how much engagement hit. QR Code below:

Views: 16,353; Engagement: 122; Celebrate Comments: 21

Argumentative Advocacy

Tara also dives deep into her inclined passion—debate forums for high school kids—by advocating for and growing the Central Florida Debate Initiative:

> "The Central Florida Debate Initiative first implemented programs in Central Florida high schools in the 2013-2014 school year. Since then, the organization has evolved into the Florida Debate Initiative in order to serve as an advocate for the development and support for speech and debate programs throughout the state. We believe that the benefits of speech and debate should be accessible to all students in our state's public, private, public charter schools and in the home school environment." –Courtesy Florida Debate Initiative

Up next: **Section 2,** where job seekers will be provisioned with a map to navigate the tumultuous job search waters. By the same token, employers, team leaders and staffing entities will amass the quiver tools to uncover hidden generational talent, leading to dynamic teams.

UPGRADE YOUR JOB OR UPGRADE YOUR PEOPLE

IDENTIFY, ENGAGE & LAND THAT IDEAL CANDIDATE OR DREAM JOB

Our roadmap provided in this section will arm digital tacticians—the candidate, the employer and the staffer—with an arsenal that will be applicable for years to come and will endure in times of milk, honey and locusts.

Hungry job seekers will be exposed to a process that packages, presents and showcases expertise and character. Similarly, CEOs and team leaders will learn to uncover and cultivate talent for their organizations, which is especially important with five generations in the workforce spanning different work styles, work ethics, interests and abilities.

Cobb Rant: Now is the time to think tactically about job hunting and recruiting. Relationship webs are smashed and the digitally diligent will benefit, while the digitally ambivalent unknowingly languish. In an antiquation predicament. Inevitable irrelevance accelerated. Heed this.

Tactical LinkedIn® Secrets was penned during the COVID-19 crisis. The 2020 Black Swan event wreaked immediate and unprecedented havoc on a scale humanity hasn't experienced since the Great Depression. In a matter of weeks, archaic paradigms shattered and LinkedIn®'s relevance accelerated around the world.

Uncertainty ravaged our global business community and revved market trends headlong into a novel normalcy, including the digitization of the B2B communication web and workforce. Unfortunately, many hardworking people also lost their jobs just as rapidly. Out of recessions and fundamental change come novel value-add opportunities. Novel enough to write about and share knowledge.

In a rapidly changing world, it's vital to have a game plan, up-to-speed skills and bankable knowledge. Those who adapt are apt—to compose their next section.

For those of us who already used technology, how fortunate. For those who did not, the need to catch up became an emergency. Overnight. Many in quarantine had time to get heads down, innovate and create a side hustle to make ends meet. If binge watching became boring, perhaps they read a book—a game plan, like this one, providing tangible knowledge to prepare for the next big, unexpected thing, as this sudden crisis will likely not be the last.

A call to action? Yes!

Job hunters and job changers, let's go to work and find you a rewarding career. Talent finders and team builders, let's identify those people and skill sets with the greatest potential for yielding success.

TOPIC 1:

THE CANDIDATE

YIELDING SUCCESS FOR JOB HUNTERS & CAREER CHANGERS

Though our "The Candidate" title bears no reference to politics (despite the movie with Robert Redford—watch it if you haven't), it sort of begs the question of how to present yourself and leverage today's platforms for the best results.

> **Cobb Rant:** Here we are advancing the real you and not smoke, mirrors and pixels. Being authentic and clear about interests, skills and your non-negotiables will take you miles in identifying, engaging and landing the dream job.

A starting point, rather a necessity, lies in exploring and executing on the power of LinkedIn® Premium. This plum LinkedIn® service offers a leg up in finding a career, in assessing available jobs and in inking the deal on the right one. It enables access to key decision makers on the org chart; and for the hiring party, it offers the promise of a wealth of talent solutions. As a candidate, be prepared to be one of the solutions, and ideally, the best one.

> Remember, prospective employers want to appear attractive to the best resource as much as the resource—or candidate—wants to attract them.

Jobs, position upgrades and unparalleled relationship-building opportunities await once your digital quiver is provisioned correctly. To reiterate: "The advice and knowledge aptly provided will prepare you with what we coin as "arrows for your digital quiver." Your quiver is an assemblage of many tools for you to apply and optimize and deploy immediately.

Cobb Rant: As you learn to navigate the digital chessboard adeptly, you will shift from archaic digital pawn to nimble queen. Options and courses of navigation will determine your success.

LinkedIn® is extremely user friendly, and the learning curve flattens quickly for smart, enterprising people across the generational spectrum. Astute minds of all ages are hopping on the technology bandwagon, and many are having the ride of their life.

THE JOB SEARCH

A common cause of anxiety is how to make some money (or a lot of it). Typically, the solution involves employment of some kind. The all-too-frequent downer is when you land the job and learn that its culture, creed or people results in unhappiness or just plain boredom.

Cobb Rant: We spend more waking hours with our co-workers and colleagues than with our families. That's a diplomatic way of saying: "You need a better job or career." Let's find some fulfillment!

DILEMMA (Job Candidate)

Your career goals are unfulfilled due to unemployment or underemployment.

Regardless of a hot or cold market, a job search should be deliberate and targeted. Fierce competition for dynamic positions now plays out on the global and virtual stage. A team leader can hire virtual assistants in India for $5 per hour. PhDs for $25 per hour. There are fewer jobs available in the crowded cyber sandbox, and bullies world over want your position.

Online archers need to focus and see through the noise. Invest at least 10 minutes a day in applying the tactical secrets below and your job search quiver will be armed, honed and primed for a win.

Whether searching for a job or trying to replace one, the first step is to step up and sign up for LinkedIn® Sales Navigator.

So sign up, place that arrow in your quiver and let's go hunting. It costs less than half a dozen Grande Lattes per month!

QUIVER IT:
JUST A LITTLE BIT!

Job candidates will learn to save ideal jobs in a digital folder and track submitted applications, while perpetually uncovering new opportunities. You will direct-message recruiters with piercing arrows, pick up salary/applicant insights and unveil who is researching you. The objective is for a targeted finesse touch to make a powerful impression leading to desired outcomes. Your quiver will deliver.

Digital LinkedIn® Quiver

Deep dive for your coveted position.

> Sign Up for LinkedIn® Sales Navigator.
> Research jobs that are available, submit your résumé and let recruiters know. You can be openly clandestine on LinkedIn®!
> Save the position in your Saved Jobs section, track Applied Jobs and turn on Job Alerts.
> Infiltrate the org chart via LinkedIn® Deep Dive. Sales Navigator is your quivered katana. Unsheath to bequeath knowledge.

➤ Look for shared connections who can make formal introductions on your behalf and add to your list of warm leads.

➤ Determine the person you would directly report to and their superiors.

➤ Identify commonalities, e.g., Scottish games, competitive eating or table tennis—or boring stuff like same alma mater.

➤ Reach out to the individual with digital arrows.

   o Non-digital touch arrows should also be deployed: the lost art of handwritten notes or, gasp, phone calls. Finally, no excuses for forgetting birthdays—and what a phenomenal touch.

Let's discuss a few tactical initiatives to get you started:

➤ Apply online.

➤ Contact a recruiter.

➤ Tactically exploit Soft Connections.

➤ Use LinkedIn® Jobs and associated functionalities.

Tactical LinkedIn® Secrets is your map to circumvent the huddled and teeming digital "application line." Regardless of what your résumé says, your document is a drop in the pixelated bucket of Word docs and PDFs sent to those who may not be the appropriate decision maker.

Cobb Rant: How do you differentiate yourself in this ocean? You don't. Differentiation amongst the masses is a fool's errand. I recommend you fish in less shark-filled and more exclusive waters. Unique warm targets are more viable and lucrative than picked-over carcasses that pass en masse as job listings.

This is where the LinkedIn® Jobs feature comes in. It lists 50M+ companies, 20M+ global job opportunities and a whopping 2M+ small businesses, the lifeline of the US economy. Trust LinkedIn® to help them hire! More and more, LinkedIn® is where employers are finding top talent and where that talent must have a presence.

LinkedIn® members with Premium subscriptions enjoy an added perk. The "Top Applicant" feature gives job searchers a leg up in identifying and applying for openings where they're triaged as a leading candidate based on their detailed profile. The feature only appears if they rank within the top 50 percent of applicants for a minimum of one position.

LINKEDIN® PRODUCTS

TACTICAL FILTERS, TIME OPTIMIZATION & TOUCHES

The LinkedIn® Products feature is a user-simple, concise and effective tool for tactical career searches and relationship building. Deploy the following arrows in your digital quiver to gain quantifiable advantages on your competitors, from organization to exposure to functionality.

> **Interview Prep** features learning videos and questions you are likely to encounter in an interview. There are multiple interactive videos, interview quizzes and tips from experts.

> **Salary Comparison** facilitates comparison analysis across industries. Don't sell your salary short by asking for less than what your colleagues are getting. Conversely, if you own a company or run a team, you want to make sure that your budget is in line with the market.

> **Résumé Writer** lists wordsmiths for hire at reasonable prices. Why try to perfect that résumé on your own when

experts and ghost writers are available and cost efficient? Mediocre résumé = mediocre job.

➢ **LinkedIn® Learning** is a masterclass series offering thousands of instructional videos with many pertaining to interviews and career searches. You can learn LinkedIn® Sales Navigator, cold calling, commercial real estate, writing with flair or even effective listening. I need that one!

➢ **LinkedIn® Groups** provides an immediate way to connect with colleagues in desired fields. Set one up to establish presence and address specific topics.

LinkedIn® Premium has potent digital search features for your arsenal. Candidates can seek open positions by using an array of filters such as compensation, geography, position(s), industry and specific organization.

Org Chart Infiltration

Aim high on the org chart and target the decisionmaker, or even better, her boss. Copy and paste imagery into a program, research each individual, positions, responsibilities, commonalities, contacts, advocacy and interests. Dig.

LinkedIn® is highly underutilized in terms of attracting return touches. Again, dig. I constantly reach out to CEOs and industry leaders on LinkedIn®. It allows me to circumvent the assistants and other time-wasting layers. Contact with a subordinate is a goose hunt. Time = dollars. Said again, dig deeper.

How do you impress decisionmakers through multiple angles and mediums?

Here's a start.

Human interaction is crucial in a rapidly digitizing business arena. In many cases, it will no longer be in person. Zoom, Skype,

Ring or the next best thing is the future of initial interviews. Once again, digital preparation is the key to success, and the first step is org chart infiltration. Scope out senior management on Linke-dIn® and visually climb down the company tree. Create your own applicable org chart with detailed notes and know the actors. I snip and paste their entire profile looking for commonalities and mutual connections. Dig and you will climb.

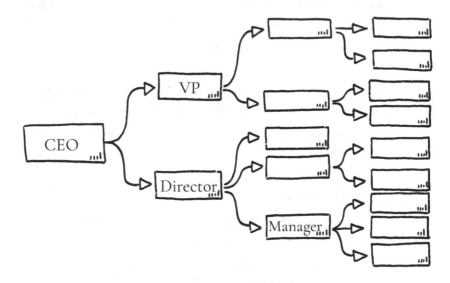

TOPIC 4:

FIRST- AND SECOND-TIER CONNECTIONS & RELATIONSHIPS

S ooner or later, you will find commonalities or interconnected relationships. Once discovered, this information can be stored in your digital quiver and released at the appropriate time. Commonalities include:

- ➢ Shared contacts
- ➢ Alumni networks
- ➢ Identical accreditations
- ➢ Participation in same LinkedIn® groups
- ➢ Membership in same professional associations
- ➢ Geographical overlap (e.g., from same hometown or country)
- ➢ Support of like-minded advocacy and philanthropic causes

Capitalize on Connections

There are three types of connections to influence your job search or career. Commonalities and relationships are the keys to capitalizing on third- and second-tier connections, which are connections outside of your everyday circle that influence your given industry. You may hear these referred to as "soft connections" or "weak ties."

Tier 1, by contrast, includes the people in your everyday life with whom you share a degree of personal and professional trust. In most cases, jobs are landed and accounts acquired through established relationships: those you know best. Tier upward for your most promising prospects.

And the countdown is on!

Tier 1

Touching the right person leads to a career path and riding the wrong horse will trot you into wasted time or a stumble-laden journey. Identifying the ideal ties must be a calculated experiment. Dynamic soft connections are the most adept and reliable arrows in your quiver and will grant you options.

Depending on your experience, networking abilities and personality, you can have thousands or dozens of direct ties in your contacts. Mentors, industry leaders and people connectors are the obvious first calls. Yes, go in for phone or digital face-to-face calls. Followed by clever and strategic digital followup. Hit targets based on priority, influence and status. Call your closest circle of contacts. Once exhausted, start finessing second-tier touches.

Tier 2

Second-tier soft connections will be introductions through an allied conduit—aka weak ties.

Create a list of allies, call them and get the conversation rolling. If the situation has legs, track the progress, follow up with your contact info and impel a warm introduction. Connectivity and introductions come from relationships in your industry and relatives at your dinner table. Friends are for finding jobs, so deploy every relationship in your networking quiver. Your competition is assuredly leveraging their relationships and nepotistic circumstances.

Tier 3

Tier 3 comprises interesting, rare, influential and resounding voices. These are the dragons and lions—relationships that will expedite digital distinction. In Section 7, we will arm you with superconnecting secrets to approach high-level relationships, practically and tactically.

> **Cobb Rant:** Seek out superconnectors and people with real influence in the business community, not the digital charlatans trumpeting their own parade. Avoid those who lack ethics and integrity. Most certainly avoid the wolves in your community. They inevitably bite. Do things right, be patient and diligent and leaders with character will gravitate your way. Cream rises. Gravy drips.

As you have learned, LinkedIn® Jobs has the cutting-edge tools necessary for you to execute on strategic job searches. Unlike any time in history, the locked filing cabinet and non-proprietary secrets no longer exist. The first step is to identify targets and expand outward. Once you engage and impress, the next goal is an interview bullseye.

> Tier 1 connections are directly accessible in your database. It's not how many people you know. It's about how many people know you and will you in your job search.

> "LinkedIn® is a valuable tool chest that allows you to really dig down and data mine to find information and contacts. You find out that people you're connected with in a professional manner share common interests, alma maters and zip codes."
> **–BILL KASKO**, PRESIDENT, FRONTLINE SOURCE GROUP

You have optimized your profile, burnished your deep dive skills and now you have successfully reached a team leader. Your cumulative efforts will lead to an interview. As ever, preparation is crucial.

LinkedIn® or LinkedOut–Tactical Differentiation

➢ Bring something of value to a leader's day with a digital touch.

➢ Share sensitive marketing intel, a well-thought-out comment to a post, links to smart time savers or relevant comic relief.

➢ Envision the world from their perch: What's keeping them up at night? How can you bust some of that stress? (Or someone's ass who trespassed against them? Okay, short rant.) What service or insight would make them feel taken care of, even if for only a touch? Look for ways to help, and make these funny, interesting, pertinent and useful.

➢ Remember, it's not about what the team leader can do for you, the solicitor, but what you, the solicitor, can do for them.

> ➤ Also bear in mind that the caliber of your gesture show-cases your caliber as a prospective hire. Treat each communication as an interview in which you're vetted as much for your potential contribution to the brain trust as for your character, discernment and likely cultural fit.
> ➤ Digital karma is an amazing phenomenon. Implement our Tactical LinkedIn® Secrets and watch your career options increase, connections jump, and interviews abound.

Time to spike the mic! Target strike with aggressive finesse and you will land an interview, whether digital or in-person.

The next section reveals the LinkedIn® hiring process through an employer's prism.

Note to the candidate: Keep reading, as you will want to take on board what your potential employer is paying attention to, and how those priorities match yours. Do your homework. Check your professional network: Anyone there who works at the organization or once did? They could give you valuable insights into the company and its hiring process.

Use this intel to determine whether the corporate culture, values and work environment are a good fit for you. Also case the company's site and social media for videos, employee testimonials, mission statements, posts about the company's recruiting efforts and other telling sources. And don't forget to read company reviews on sites such as Glassdoor, CareerBliss, Vault, TrustPilot and the Better Business Bureau.

No red flags? Excellent. Now start prepping for your interviews. Once hiring managers are identified, you must deep dive key social platforms. Instagramify, Twitter-dive and TikTokit till you're armed with the necessary info to ace that interview.

> "My advice to young people is to interview their prospective employers and perform a deep dive into their digital résumé."
> –DAVID COBB

THE EMPLOYER

YIELDING SUCCESS FOR THE EMPLOYER

Understanding your target candidate and being clear on the needed competencies and cultural fit for your company and teams will allow for strategically planned empathic interaction. It is the foundation of knowing whom to select, engage, woo or deny.

The following section addresses tactics for employers to find an ideal candidate and integrate them into dynamic organizations.

DILEMMA (Employers & Teams)

People with talent and character are hard to find.

> "One arrow alone can easily be broken but many arrows are indestructible." –GENGHIS KHAN

As a team leader during what was considered a hot real estate market, our company wasn't focused on talent acquisition by design. Candidates were too expensive and some naively arrogant.

Like any entrepreneurial archer, we experienced digital hits and misses. The same applied to job seekers.

The motto at Archon Commercial Advisors is: "Hire Slow, Fire Fast." We have been very selective about talent in down markets and even pickier when the market is *en fuego*. The dynamic changed in the wake of coronavirus, as markets dramatically shifted and tactically prepared organizations glimpsed the deluge of potential hires.

There's no time like the present to augment your team and attract key talent from your competition. If you empathically onboard the competition's executors, ingrained relationships are sure to follow, inviting empathy among the employees and future competitors' employees you may want to hire. It will be easy pickings against digitally shortsighted opponents. They won't even know why they are losing.

> **Cobb Rant:** The chessboard is yours as the queen, but you need knights, bishops, rooks and even pawns to win the game. When you take a key piece from a nemesis, industry colleagues not only notice, but they celebrate, advocate and propagate, through engagement.

This not only augments your competitive edge but diminishes that of your digital-chess nemesis. High-level business is survival of the fittest, and hobbling and checkmating rule the chess tournament. When strategic personnel are lifted from a myopic contender, attention share is pilfered to thunderous applause—Likes, Celebrates, Supports, Loves, Insightfuls and Curious on LinkedIn®. The talented individual's association with the previous organization is swiftly forgotten as the world turns ever onward.

> Capitalize on relationships (appropriately), dominate your competition and put them in the rearview mirror.

In the interview and hiring process, every employer will encounter the characteristics of candidates as those described below. The checkmate is when there is clarity on the skill set that is identified as the best fit and vested in a role that will offer success for both the company and the candidate. Target the king while operating like the queen. Load LinkedIn® on your chessboard and Tactical LinkedIn® Secrets will be your digital cannon. Pick your targets on the board, aim and fire.

COBB'S CHESSBOARD
- King—lumbering, rigid and has influence
- Queen—adept and nimble with options
- Bishop—the queen's right-hand executor or key person
- Knight—unique skillset, executor or specialist
- Rook—infantry or role play
- Pawn—inconsequential, bumbling and can be used as cannon fodder. (Okay, who really wants to be cannon fodder…?)

> "God is on the side of the heaviest cannon."
> **–NAPOLEON BONAPARTE**

If a job seeker understands solutions to problems, they will land the position with a head start up the career ladder. If they can take initiative and be proactive, those candidates are possible game changers.

LINKEDIN® JOBS

APPLICABLE APPS & FEATURES

There is a method to the madness of getting to the right resource. Begin by using the LinkedIn® Sales Navigator feature and mining its benefits:

➤ **Post a job** and you will receive immediate résumé submissions.

➤ **Talent Solutions** is a paid service for the precise targeting of candidates.

➤ **Salary Comparison**, as explained above, will keep your salary negotiations in line with market conditions.

➤ **LinkedIn® Learning**, also per the above, is an excellent application for existing and new employees who could use some guidance in content creation, résumé writing and the like. In an upcoming discussion, we'll address LinkedIn® Learning as a lab for creating masterclass videos, webinars and seminars.

A team leader should deploy all germane resources to find critical talent. Any machine is only as good as the sum of its parts, and the same is applicable to B2B competition on LinkedIn®. One talented person only has X number of hours, Y amount of energy and Z amount of creativity. Put the right team in place, and X + Y + Z creates a triple force multiplier of productivity and creativity. The long-term goal for a true leader should be for the organization to survive beyond any individual's leadership longevity, including the founder. Whom do you need and whom are you developing in your leadership and employee pipeline so that the business thrives without their abilities and positioning? Short-sighted digital strategies lead to team growth stagnation and eventual organizational demise. If you aren't digitally growing, you are digitally dying, which dooms your offline longevity as well.

TACTICAL APPLICATION:
WRITE A BLOG—NINJA MARKETING

Do you need a blog as a marketing asset? Indeed, you do.

As a team, surely you are smart enough to write a good blog, but are you organized enough or do you have time enough to write 52 per year and balance a career? The right team dynamic turns a simple blog into a cost-free, dynamic and deployable marketing asset.

> **Cobb Rant:** Despite a busy schedule, there are ways to streamline your creativity that bear results, but you must assemble the right ninjas. Those ninjas are your team members who are capable of leveraging content and the knowledge you have imparted. Tap them to help generate or own the writing and syndicating of the blog and companion media efforts.

Analysis of team roles is the crux. Who is the best at writing what? How to ensure a diversity of backgrounds and POVs? The intention is to harness strengths that can most closely exact match your strategic communications needs.

Time to tactically identify and analyze your ninjas:

> **Team Member #1 (Organizer)**—Possesses organizational, management and daily business operations skills (Catalog Imagery, Calendar Content and Run Team). This team member is adept at posting all forms of imagery and media and understands digital communication.

> **Team Member #2 (Creative)**—Possesses creative energy and communications skills (Content Author, Melds Business/Creative Process). These are the writers and video storytellers with a knack for creative processes. They're the dreamers and idea peeps, and they generate positivity with a flair.

> **Team Member #3 (Closer)**—Is an established industry expert who spends time generating revenue and whose adventures in writing rarely go beyond business plans. This team member, or members, can be a little difficult to get off the creative bench, but will enjoy scoring engagement points once they see what LinkedIn® can do for their business.

> **Team Member #4 (The Creative Closer)**—This is where you become the queen of the LinkedIn® chessboard. Few people execute inside and outside the LinkedIn® labyrinth. They either lack the expertise or tech savvy. As you will recall, the queen is adept and nimble, with options. Creative closers are constantly creating, deploying and optimizing their process through team dynamics executed by dynamic teams. People.

TOPIC 7:

TEAM BUILDING

AND LINKEDIN® TALENT SOLUTIONS

Recruiting is the first step in team building and is a path to competitive dominance. There is no other medium with the sweeping capabilities of LinkedIn®, which was designed as a job search website.

> Approximately 80 percent of B2B leads derive from LinkedIn®, as compared to Twitter at 13 percent.

The forum is comprehensive, teeming with thinkers and robust in terms of talented chess pieces available. Traverse the crowd to find the right bishop, rook, knight or pawn for your team.

Cobb Rant: Resources abound for the reciprocal discovery of talent and positions. LinkedIn® Talent Solutions provides precise tools for scooping up ninjas.

Whatever the B2B segment you operate in, technological skills and an open-minded attitude towards tech-based learning should influence hiring decisions.

TACTICAL APPLICATION:
BILL KASKO, PRESIDENT, FRONTLINE SOURCE GROUP

Bill Kasko's company places temporary staffing and high-level office professionals. In my conversation with him, he recalled:

"When the hurricane hit Houston a few years ago, there was terrible flooding and dislocation of animals. We got a phone call from the American Society for the Prevention of Cruelty to Animals (ASPCA). They needed 50 people to assist in walking and feeding 30,000 dogs and cats that were abandoned or lost. We put people to work who'd lost their jobs, and it went on for nine months. LinkedIn® allowed us to figure it out and showed us a different way to do things.

"As the pandemic hit Texas, we began placing people at testing centers throughout the state. As FEMA pulls out, our 700 employees will be the ones on the front line—for once I get to use this correctly! We're not in health care. But we were tapped on the shoulder and told, 'You guys came recommended as being able to pull this off. Can you do it?'

"LinkedIn® has allowed us to continue to figure out how to move forward as things change, from getting new clients, to obtaining new relationships, to finding the right candidates, to building those relationships. Some of the people we placed were clients before. And then they came to us or they moved to another company and we went with them. Or we placed them with a company and then they became a hiring manager and then we got an update saying, 'Hey, congratulations on your promotion.' And when we reached out, we went, 'You're a hiring manager; guess what, now you're a client!'

> "LinkedIn® is an incredible tool if you figure out how to use it. And that's the key. You just have to figure it out."

"Since Microsoft bought LinkedIn®, the analytics inform us to make the best decisions about how, when and where we invest, and allow us to try things that we've never been able to try before. It's functional data that we can really jump into and manipulate to figure out models and what is going to pay from an ROI perspective."

Digital LinkedIn® Quiver
LinkedIn® Talent Solutions
➢ Post a Job Position to 675M+ Candidates
➢ Apply 20+ Smart Search Filters
➢ Activate Increased InMail Capabilities
➢ Manage Talent & Create a Pipeline

Technological Interview Preparation

As much as you think the candidate needs you, they are also interviewing your tech adeptness. Don't assume that every candidate who walks into that door is sold on your organization, especially if your competition has a stronger digital presence. Truly talented candidates typically have multiple options—technology trumps legacy.

KEYS TO EXECUTION

Opportunistic scenarios can quickly shift to incremental, fundamental and detrimental dilemmas if an organization sits on its hands. The next generation of capable performers will be forward thinking and tech adept. Technology and other socio-economic variables are catalyzing trends at an astounding rate—including the inevitable demise of digitally myopic organizations. Employ the features detailed above to land generational talent, accelerate down-market growth and build a lucrative organization. You have just completed Sections 1 and 2 of *Tactical LinkedIn® Secrets*.

You added to your digital quiver with:

➢ **Your Guide to Competitive Dominance**—Building Relationships, Status & Wealth

➢ **Upgrade Your Job or Upgrade Your People**—Identify, Engage & Land that Ideal Candidate or Dream Job

Read on... **Section 3** will equip you to pivot, brand build and establish prominence as well as to harness brainpower, innovate solutions and dominate adversaries.

These secrets will bring you to the next tier of digital adeptness and reverse the effects of conformist, conventional and collective thinking. True differentiation will unlock your creative potential.

DIGITAL PERCEPTION IS REALITY

PIVOT, BRAND-BUILD & ESTABLISH PROMINENCE

"If you are afraid of failure, you don't deserve to be successful."

–Charles Barkley (NBA Legendary Rebounder)

The tides of digital change are cresting, and a new generation of dynamic business leaders needs to choose between *The Titanic* and Michael Phelps. In other words, do you want to sink or swim?

Buoyancy + Agility = Ability to Pivot.

As an undersized power forward, I used the pivot as one of the most subtly lethal weapons in my strategic basketball arsenal. A classic hardwood pivot is about adaptation, position and getting to the ball first. In this section of *Tactical LinkedIn® Secrets*, you will learn how to pivot, technologically rebound and take market share in your given industry or organization—first to the ball and in a Barkelyesque fashion.

> **Cobb Rant:** If you are snoozing, you are losing, but *Tactical LinkedIn® Secrets* will fix that with one dynamic pivot. This pivot will require a change in attitude toward technology and acceptance that your digital perception is reality. Silicon Valley expansion was already a wildfire of game-changing innovation, affecting trends globally.

The pandemic of 2020 accelerated trends, and smartphone addiction has amplified the number of hours humans stare at screens.

> Your adversaries/competitors are waking up to a newly created horizon of competition, and they want the sunshine. The received rays are attention marketshare!

By reading this far, you are ready to get in the game, and now it's time to hone your tactical digital skills. In (more or less) the words of Ice Cube, pass yourself the pill and let's shake the comp through creative flanking, then *slam dunk it like Shaquille O'Neal.*

TOPIC 1:

THE CREATIVE-TACTICAL MIND

The pill? A nickname for a basketball, and once you take control of your game, it's liberating. As a high-level commercial real estate entrepreneur, I thrive in chaos, run hard with the bulls and treasure executed initiatives.

I was running crazy hard a few years ago, even by my standards. In the thick of the slog, I was reminded that the fastest racehorses have blinders. Those deal sprints led to multiple lucrative years, but in many cases I was blinded by paying too much attention to what others were doing. That's okay, many people, including me, need focus blinders at times to focus.

Cobb Rant: Whether trotting, galloping or striding, focus blinders can help you. But they can also shut out your external stimuli and creativity. The chase for money and repetitive tasks will pull you into an uncreative and dark chasm. It's a balancing act for sure. Put on the right blinders to illuminate and sharpen your innate ability to create.

Resounding Pivots & Getting Your Mojo Going

I have met so many people who say the following:

➤ "I don't know where to start on LinkedIn®."
➤ "I'm too busy with job responsibilities to post on Linke-dIn®."
➤ "I'm not creative enough to post on LinkedIn®."

First off, these sayings are complete BS. Let's delineate where to start and launch with minimal time engagement vs. time guzzlers that would compromise daily job responsibilities. The proclamations above are nothing more than tepid excuses that automatons deploy against an invisible and inevitable trend in LinkedIn®.

Secondly, you will learn to harness your tactical creativity. This will lead to fulfilling, passionate and dynamic content. Every human being has the potential to become an expert. Expertise entwined with creativity will optimize your tactical and digitally artistic modus operandi.

As with everything else in life, you can't make a three pointer without getting started diligently and deliberately. I want to warn you now that if you slack off in the preparation process, this isn't the book for you. In my world, you start what you finish. If you don't put the time in, you will fall and fail. Fall behind and fail to keep up with your digital competition. Your personal brand will remain veiled while others' flourish online.

Your entire life is about to change. There are many ways to unleash creativity and passion. Once you find these, the road is easy. Finding the white rabbit is the tough part, especially if efforts don't yield magic immediately. You have to cut your teeth on LinkedIn®, and it's tough to eat while cutting your teeth. In the words of my executive coach, sage Dwight Bain, "Feed LinkedIn® and It Will Feed You." So why isn't everyone slaying it on LinkedIn®?

Cobb Rant: One word: complacency. We all fight it. My biggest fear is that you read *Tactical LinkedIn® Secrets* and not treat our lessons as crucial to your win. We will teach you to avoid creativity blocks and begin a full-court press to all-star performance. A veritable slam dunk.

"Things turn out best for the people who make the best of the way things turn out." **–COACH JOHN WOODEN**

Functional Creativity

"Once my Broncos teammates and coaches taught me the strategy behind watching film. The preparation. I was always ready for a tactical battle." **–JOHN MOBLEY** (FORMER NFL LINEBACKER & 2X SUPERBOWL CHAMPION)

How do you fuse tactical applications with creative projects? It's a three-step process: Preparation, Serendipitous Research and Creative Implementation.

➢ **Preparation**—Preparation is the Air Jordan you need to become a champ. If you don't control your time, life will inevitably pull you in random and wasteful directions. Keep your eye on the scoreboard. Consider LinkedIn® time to be as critical as a meeting with a potential new client or your boss. Distracted complacency is your biggest threat. Prepare and you won't have to repair—your digital reputation, that is! As a high-level basketball player, I always scouted the other team. Looked at their plays and learned from their strategy. And why not steal a few ideas on social media, quiver them, make them unique and warm up to release? The goal is to handle the ball. Pass along the strong posts till you get in your groove. Enmesh, emulate and execute.

➢ **Serendipitous Research**—Rabbit holes lead to other rabbit holes and twist into areas one tier outside your expertise. Cultivate knowledge in adjacent fields and broaden your network, skill set and purview. Explore. Your contacts will increase and so will your creative brainpower. An ancillary benefit is that you will e-meet and meet people who are game to learn, earn and collaborate.

➢ **Creative Implementation**—This involves psychology and tranquility. There are more hurdles than just banging keys. The mind must be undistracted. It doesn't matter if you are irked at the headlines, are brawling with a family member or constantly summoned to domestic responsibilities, your mind is distracted. When said annoying distractions happens, it makes it very tough to write or be disciplined to write posts, update your profile or communicate with others who may up your game.

Digital LinkedIn® Quiver: Drills

➢ Allocate time to organize your thoughts.

➢ Create your content and enlist your team's input.

➢ Organize a content calendar. The right functional calendar will offer services ranging from prompting, managing and distributing your content to facilitating responses and crunching metrics. I advise that you plan two to three weeks out. Calendar recommendation: Loomly. https://www.loomly.com

➢ Write to influence. Creativity, deliberate application and deadlines will whip complacency to the bench.

TOPIC 2:

CREATIVITY AMID CHAOS

D eadlines, doctor appointments, work dramas, survival training, home schooling, Zoom calls, work outs, meditation, political powwows—all are inevitable distractions or responsibilities, depending on a person's lens. We all have daily squirrels (distractions), but deliberately focused time is the *sine qua non* of effective creativity.

> For those of us who do not speak Latin, *sine qua non* means an essential condition; a thing that is absolutely necessary.

Distraction = Ineffective Creativity

The recipe for creativity contains key ingredients, including a big splash of rigidity. How can creativity be rigid? Through focused time.

Pursue rigid creative time on LinkedIn®. The first step is knowing when your thinking and abilities peak. Hydration is vital to mental function, and exercise acts as a natural brain stimulant. All watered and pumped? Now you're ready to feed your faculties.

Many creatives are at their best early morning or late at night, but everyone is different. The mind must be rested, active and not distracted.

> "Creativity is intelligence having fun." –ALBERT EINSTEIN

Setting the stage for ideas to flow takes purposeful preparation. Begin by tapping into varied sources of knowledge and data. An easy way is to bookmark a diverse assortment of LinkedIn® articles and blogs. Just be sure to go beyond your profession.

Enrich your repertoire of insights and inspiration by reaching across genres as diverse as sports and culture, finance and medicine, outer space and inner psychology. Or maybe advocacy and spirituality are more your thing. Whatever stokes your imagination and can switch on that content lightbulb deserves time and shelf room in your digital library.

All set? Now find a quiet place and rigidly employ and deploy creativity. It's a path to peace and prosperity.

Cobb Rant: Caution: If you view LinkedIn® content creation as a mundane task, your message will not reverberate with your audience. Approach LinkedIn® as a chance to harvest your creativity and yield a lush digital cornucopia. Find a regimented time and stick to it.

> Do not let distractions distract.

Uncreative Landmines

As you begin to master the art of the arrows, your peers will undoubtedly notice. Internally and externally, your success will illuminate strengths and generate beneficial impressions. And if you're really kicking ass and taking down prospect emails, you're bound to ruffle some feathers. Expect to find new friends and uncover dormant enemies. It's an inevitable part of your journey.

Novice digital archers come to me all the time with tales of being flamed by envy arrows. I'll share a few examples of pointed barbs you may receive someday and a few of my ready responses. Below are a handful of real-world whammies fired off by threatened peers or colleagues. Don't endure the insecure.

> **Cobb Rant:** Friends and mentees often consult me when passive-aggressive questions turn up. Nothing annoys me more than a Negative Nancy-or-Nick-Naysayer attempting to dim a budding creative's shimmer.

Here are a few scenarios.

One toxic salvo was aimed at Marti Weinstein, my homegirl whose Tactical Application we highlighted earlier in *Tactical LinkedIn® Secrets*. Remember, Marti is less experienced in business, LinkedIn® and life. She's a rookie in her 20s, a phenomenal young go-getter—and we've all been there. This guy got me going. That poor malcontent wrote to my protégé:

Q: Why are you posting on LinkedIn® instead of doing deals?

When Marti told me, I shook my head and responded with counter-indignance: "They're jealous that you are freaking killing it! Keep going, girl. One day, you'll be looking down on the dinosaurs from the leadership podium."

To quote Agent Smith from *The Matrix*, "That's the sound of inevitability." And they have no idea how inevitable things will become. Marti is resilient and deflective, and we will continue to chart her hard-knocks journey and newly attained digital prowess. She's amassing accreditations as the T-Rexes undergo fossilization.

Below is another gem I heard when I first started writing edgy content and creating videos:

Q: Are you trying to be an influencer or something?

I've gotten this myself a few times and know other creatives catch similar envy arrows from struggling colleagues. Everyone can find a reasonable level of creativity with a modest amount of work and concerted thought. Not everyone breathes helium, but hyper-critical content consumers could use a hit of humility. Stuck in the past and cowed by the future, they defend their turf with conventionality and stagnation. Let their comments slide off your back like raindrops on your rear window as they fade away.

Newsflash: Even though the small minority of detractors can be loud, you will rarely encounter them face to face. Be strong, fix people's problems, cultivate empathy and you will always be able to score, rebound and pivot. No matter how strong the opponent or how devastating the loss. Plus you can always block or just be "delete'n the cretins." (Cobbism)

INADEQUATE DIGITAL PRESENCE VS. COMPETITION

Your LinkedIn® posts cannot be air balls. Keep your arc high and sink them in the net. Period. Below is a scenario where I bet you can empathize.

Cobb Rant: You wake up, a little dehydrated, hangry and grumpily start your day. It's early and you haven't repaid your sleep debt. You stretch, take the phone off the charger and check out your LinkedIn®. That's becoming a routine and you know it! Just own it.

Unlike morning habits of decades past such as reading the daily paper, interactive content consumption often happens before users attain full consciousness. Our shiny screens serve as an alarm clock and an information depot. Many users greet LinkedIn® before knocking out eye boogers and morning breath. That's the power of LinkedIn®—waking and sleeping impressions, as cyclical as the moon and sun. Within seconds of rousing, our neural pathways lead us directly to our digital addiction.

You glimpse headlines, ping the weather app and open your LinkedIn® feed. Boom, what? A competitor like me drops an engagement bomb across your relationship web. Positive tar and feathers. What do I mean by a bomb?

DIGITAL COMPETITION QUIVER–POST MOVES

A dynamic and fun way to measure engagement is with the basketball metric. Let's compare post vs. post in this digital roundball showdown:

POST #1: DYNAMIC NETWORKING
➤ 4,835 Views
➤ 59 Likes (59 Points)
➤ 2 Hovers (4 points)
➤ 5 Comments (15 points)
➤ 0 ResharesTotal Hoops Metric Score = 78 points

POST #2: GAMESTOP JANET GALVIN
➤ 2,510 Views
➤ 44 Likes (44 Points)
➤ 7 Hovers (14 Points)
➤ 8 Comments (24 Points)
➤ 0 ResharesTotal Hoops Metric Score = 82 points

Analysis: Janet wins by a four-point margin with a strong 82 points. The reason was because we invested in a trending infographic that played on the Gamestop investing frenzy. The dynamic networking pic was right behind due to strong imagery and positive energy. Both elicit expertise and fun—what more could you ask for.

Engagement

Engagement is significant! The typical alpha contender wants to be in the center of action, and LinkedIn® is perpetual movement play by play. While you're limbering up, the effective and dominant players are dropping dynamic content all over your existing and prospective relationship web. Sticky content. Your competition is winning, by default, if you are on the bench.

So how do winners know they are winning? They keep score, silly! You can't win without minding the tally, and *Tactical LinkedIn® Secrets* will teach you tactical quantification. How, you ask? The answer is plain: the ever-popular emoji.

➢ **Likes:** Only clicks required.

➢ **Hover Emojis: Celebrate / Love / Insightful / Curious / Support**

➢ **Comments:** Requires thinking, writing and putting yourself out there.

➢ **Reshare:** The ultimate compliment is for a colleague to distribute your intellectual content to their following.

You down your caffeine and peruse your feed as loads of coveted relationships interconnect with the top strivers in your field. Those strivers are feeding off one another's strategies, energies and synergies. In other words, the competition is whipping your ass. It's the feeling that the opponents of Central Florida hoops legend Vince Carter experienced just before he slammed a gravity-defying, above-the-rim dunk tip dunk. Gravity knocked me out of orbit as he defied it. I got dominated. But at least I was in the game and not a spectator. And I quickly reentered the space and never gave up. Ask him.

It's a great story, and one of the only times I've ever felt completely helpless and bested in a serious playoff. You do not want to be in that position or even worse, a non-participant on LinkedIn®.

Case in Point: Yours Truly—David Cobb

I experienced similar helplessness when I first did a deep dive into LinkedIn®. Back then I had just under 1,000 followers and thought my profile was great because it showed "500+ Connections." How naive. It was time to tackle LinkedIn® with the tenacity that I approach all serious competition, but I realized I needed a coach. I picked my team knowing I'd need to roll with the punches.

Initial guidance came from my ninja executive coach, Dwight Bain. As my thinking evolved, I sought out an ally and expert in Alex Cervasio. His firm, CVAS Consulting, helped me lay the tracks for what led to over 5 million views, a 20-fold increase in followers. But most importantly, it led to rapidly accelerating engagement. Engagement is your key to success. Not views.

You've noticed that this section has a basketball theme, and in the spirit of my favorite game, I created a tracking system for your digital quiver based on basketball scoring. There are four ways to score on a basketball play. A free throw is worth one point, and a layup is worth two. A shooter can also score three points from behind the three-point arc. The crown jewel is, if fouled in the act of shooting a three pointer, a player can hit the shot, convert a free throw and make the ever-elusive four-point play.

Let's use the four-tiered Hoops Engagement Metric to highlight why engagement matters more than views. Your content must emotionally resonate with your readers. If you touch their hearts and minds, they will engage, and you will impress. Positive impressions lead to relationship acquisition. Let's arm your digital quiver and dominate like Vinsanity*, only on LinkedIn®.

*As Vince Carter fans know, his famous gravity-defying dunks led to the term "Vinsanity."

TOPIC 4:

ILLUMINATE & DOMINATE

We've armed your quiver with prowess and metrics. It's time to compete. Stack your content into a calendar and identify your audience, because you are now a digital archer and writer. Let's deploy some arrows. Begin by researching stories, historical context or other digital info to share. Just make them yours by adding your spin.

> **Cobb Rant:** Stockpile, stack, send, repeat. Load yourself up with content and distribution will occur with ease. Once you distribute, you can compare, measure and compete. Don't be scared. Analyze how you stack up against your competitors. Use our basketball metric and traditional engagement formula to keep up with the digital Joneses. Talk a little smack to your annoying neighbors. It can be fun.

It's not about huge numbers initially. That's the pro league. No one is entitled to begin in the NBA. You have to climb to play above the rim. Low initial numbers and incremental follower growth are the process required to cultivate a successful foundation for execution. You must develop fundamentals before you can slam dunk.

Digital LinkedIn® Quiver

➢ Target engagement through sharing knowledge from personal experiences or published and cited insights from other digital authors. (Yes, you are a digital *auteur* now.)

➢ Research and follow specific news stories and trends on LinkedIn®.

➢ Pick & roll - Pick your most dynamic content, roll out in a timely, opportune way and provide commentary in written and video formats.

➢ Use the Saved Items section.

➢ See how you compare to your competition through our Hoops Engagement Metric. Plug in your stats and add up basketball points.

Actions speak louder than words. So we'll spin a tale of an industry leader-turned-digital-marketing archer. His name is Mike Guggenheim, and he quickly recognized the importance of LinkedIn® marketing. He was one of my first ninja digital guinea pigs.

TACTICAL APPLICATION:
THE GUGGENHEIM EXPERIMENT_

Mike Guggenheim has been a great friend and commercial real estate confidante. Reciprocal sound boarding is the communication dynamic for most of our conversations. Early on we discussed authorship, and he not only complimented my foresight in writing industry blogs—he was intrigued.

That was refreshing because a few of my CRE (commercial real estate) colleagues ridiculed me for wanting to be a "Writer/Influencer." Envy barbs are the best sign that you are at the forefront. If what you are doing doesn't matter, the invisible "they" wouldn't care or talk about you.

Mike realized that my writing was having an impact on our industry, and some articles resonated with him emotionally. We started brainstorming ideas. I showed him my creative writing process for enmeshing analytical creativity with real-world subject matter. He just jumped off the cliff and started landing a couple of blogs a month. Synthesizing insights from his daily operations, Mike showed that he's executing on initiatives, is a leader and has the power to reach internal and outside influencers with a message of positivity. Plus he's always good for a laugh. And he gets me into his museum for free. #mikesnudeportraitisamazing

We're both still savoring a LinkedIn® think piece we co-authored several months before the pandemic hit stateside. Entitled *3 Predictions: Problems CRE Owners Will Face in 2020 & Expert Solutions*, it anticipated trends we saw looming on the commercial real estate horizon as we broached a new year and a new decade. Here are a few excerpts:

Dave's Prediction:

"Retailers will close locations, ask for rent reductions and aggressively negotiate renewals. It will become a more Tenant-Friendly Commercial Real Estate market."

Mike's solution:

"Identify Local Occupancy Threats—Identify high-risk tenants and categorize them. There are always regional/local tenants who will fail. Identify them through proactive communication among tenant, leasing agent and property management. On a side note, some good-hearted people start businesses that fail. If you get ahead of the situation, the departure can lessen the small business owner's financial loss—which doesn't make an agent or [landlord] money but is the right thing to do."

Mike's Prediction:

"When [recessions] occur, owners and landlords will have to adjust their pricing, deal with lender events, adapt to the landscape or lose their property. In many cases, the fallout of a few key tenants creates a cash flow domino effect that ultimately results in a default event."

Dave's Solution:

"Favor Credit & Co-Tenancy vs. ROI: If you have a tenant fallout, a solid leasing agent will aim to replace them quickly and with a strong financially backed tenant. In many cases, this means backfilling at a lower rate. It's not an enjoyable experience for the [landlord], but in a down market, it's a necessary evil. CREDIT & TERM ARE MORE VALUABLE THAN RENT!!!"

With responses such as "Spot on Projections" and "thanks for sharing this practical business wisdom," our article sparked Mike's followers. He went from the hundreds to more than 6,700 followers and dozens of new and dynamic relationships in just over 1 year.

Initially, I illustrated how to strategically grow a targeted following. Then we went in for consistent and dynamic content distribution. Mike identified his core competencies and strengths to accentuate on LinkedIn®. He has since written numerous blogs and found a hidden passion for writing. Similar to my CRE office, Guggenheim Commercial has bonded through publishing on LinkedIn®.

Mike opened up his creative-tactical mind and put in place a protocol, and helping hands, to keep the content wheels whirring. This meant hiring a dedicated team to schedule and research articles so he and his associates could "be engaged on multiple formats on a regular basis."

Beyond word slinging, they've expanded into audiovisual. Topics have included the challenges of closing deals during shutdown and, once the restrictions were lifted, the impact of restrictions and mandates on markets and properties. These are but two of their pandemic-era videos that garnered plaudits and analytics around the country.

As Mike explained, "C-level executives and leasing agents are looking and listening to us, and we're getting work as a result of it." He stressed the power of sharing ideas on LinkedIn® to build B2B brands and networks. Because the old way of doing biz, he knows, is history.

"During my 30-year real estate career, relationships have evolved from networking meetings, conferences and cold calling to individual branding in developing a robust, value-driven, social media platform—LinkedIn® being the dominant platform in B2B and commercial real estate that allows users to cast a significantly wider net in developing relationships. Even that guy who's going to the golf club and thinks he's going to get all that business, if he's not a thought leader on LinkedIn® or some platform, when he's meeting with these guys, they're going to say, 'Well, we're going with the guy we read every single day and who actually has great thoughts, great ideas, and you're sitting here doing nothing but playing golf. You're not bringing any value; you're not bringing anything to the table. Digital engagement offers a unique way to get underneath everybody's skin… How many people can you touch? How can you provide some value to those people? And how do you create your own voice without sounding too redundant? That's what's important." –MIKE GUGGENHEIM

KEYS TO EXECUTION

Will you be LinkedIn® or LinkedOut?

Cobb Rant: Now is the time to step up your digital game. Don't be boring, and let's start scoring.

As we discussed, you must get focused and avoid pitfalls and distractions. If you ignore the negativity and invest yourself in the process, you might just find a new passion or calling. As this book progresses, we will challenge you, just as coaches and mentors challenged me. The next section is your last stretch of digital basic training. *Tactical LinkedIn® Secrets* will further hone your creativity to a razor-sharp edge, allowing for a penetrating and targeted touch arrow from a well-armed quiver at the optimum time.

Question? What is a penetrating touch arrow? What I mean by this is dynamic, incisive and influential writing. There's still room in your digital quiver for a few more dynamic and potent tools. You will write to influence. So pull out the quiver and let's acquire some new weapons.

TARGETED NICHES & BRAND DIFFERENTIATION

NICHES LEAD TO EXPERT STATUS & RICHES

"Eventually you will hit upon a particular field, niche or opportunity that suits you perfectly. You will recognize it when you find it because it will spark that childlike sense of wonder and excitement; it will feel right."
–Robert Greene (Ninja author of *Mastery*)

You can't target the indefinable masses or your message will be a drip in the digital tsunami. In this chapter we will explore and dissect the dynamics and advantages of niche discernment. Creatively create contrast from your colleagues, competition and dominate smaller rooms. You'll eventually kick down doors to more expansive realms and higher levels of amazing relationships.

TOPIC 1:

BLUE OCEAN

B lue ocean connotates business, brand and personal opportunity. The term indicates the need to think outside of the tank. What will be your "widget," or the next big thing others will choose to buy?

Blue ocean innovation can lead to the development of new enterprises or the reinvention of existing ones. These ingeniously designed and strategized initiatives, for profit or not, are novel ways to earn, employ, engage and in a nutshell, change the landscape of how we operate in the world. Maybe you are the next person to create the new trend, technology, tool or solution to daily needs that we now grapple with or at least about which we are now aware.

Hegemonization Leads to Homogenation

Dominance breeds uniformity. Progressive thinking, when it yields a winning solution, leads to the new big thing.

Think Uber, cars booked on your screen. Think Netflix and its impact on Blockbuster. (Imagine trudging out to a store for a VHS tape!) Think digital cameras—the dark room really went dark with their illumination on screens.

For its part, LinkedIn® has handed professional headhunters their hats. Such occupational hazards can't be helped as traditional mediums give way to the new.

Food for thought: LinkedIn® has methodically homogenized (hegemonized) the career development and professional networking industry. The joint LinkedIn®-Microsoft force field is hegemonizing traditional communication channels with astounding efficiency, creating a uniform mega-platform.

> **Cobb Rant:** It's the Big Bang innovation of the employment universe and it's only expanding. Find other intelligent life out there and connect with new ideas, people and opportunities.

Exploring the Waters of LinkedIn®

Whether it concerns commercial space travel, upgrading to driverless cars, depositing checks through our phones or receiving groceries via drones, the horizon of adaptation is infinite. Think of it as the vast blue sea or the big blue marble. The world as your oyster. Ingenuity equals marketshare.

For corporations, entrepreneurs and job hunters, the blue ocean within LinkedIn® is an ecosystem that impacts business development and the know-how to build a profitable career.

Jonathan "Jon" Hellein is more than a business partner. He's family to me. We've been through ups, downs, tears, jeers and cheers. We've executed on some serious initiatives and like to play with the lions—no kittens or hyenas, please. I couldn't be more thankful for Jon and Janet as my partners. As you can see from our website— always personalize your brand and tag with humanistic photos.

There are no two people the world I want more in my trio of trenches: LinkedIn®, authorship and swim-with-the-sharks commercial real estate. Sharks are always circling at higher levels. Meaning, they are going to take a bite out of your business or credibility. It makes the colosseum more interesting.

> No matter the predators, LinkedIn® remains a blue ocean.

Jon and I have adeptly executed in the CRE red ocean shark tanks. These are markets that are overdeveloped and saturated. To survive, we have been proactive and constantly evolved and reinvented ourselves. LinkedIn® and digital authorship were catalysts of and a showcase for our collaborative and solo reinventions.

Plus, we quit ordering Krystal cheeseburgers to our dive-bar strategy sessions, and both shed some pounds pretty fast. Kind of like Oprah in the '90s. Jon and I joke about everything. Life is too serious to be too serious.

Conversely, we've also been known to spar a little. We had a few severe bouts over our LinkedIn® strategy. Yet, disagree as we may have on details such as how to approach content, we never once clashed on the fundamental premise that LinkedIn® is crucial. Later in the section "Jon's Tactical Application," we reveal a fuller discussion of our differing views and Jon's ensuing decision points and success.

TOPIC 2:

THE NICHE PIVOT

Have you heard the term jack-of-all-trades and master of none? That phrase could not be more applicable to the LinkedIn® theater of competition. Get extra butter popcorn for the opening round.

Cobb Rant: There are three rules to this high-stakes game: Specialize, specialize, specialize. Sharpen your arrowhead or prepare to meet your inevitable demise. Quiver, aim, release! The first objective of your "bullet point" (arrowhead in LinkedIn®-ese) is to clarify what your brand does, and why.

A personal brand cannot be everything to everyone. LinkedIn® is not Kim Kardashian's Twitter or Justin Bieber's Instagram. LinkedIn® is designed for high-level business initiatives. Arm your quiver and govern it accordingly.

Let's Quiver-Niche, just a little bit.

Nook Initiatives

I sat down with Alex Cervasio, founder of CVAS Consulting, when I retained him for a social media campaign for the Ty Cobb Museum. His social marketing prowess will be showcased in the forthcoming advocacy section. I told Alex I recognized the power of LinkedIn® and wanted to have a voice. I needed, and heeded, his advice.

Tactical Conversation (okay, the Cliff's Notes):

Dave: I think having a voice on LinkedIn® will help my business. What should I do?

Alex: Demonstrate your expertise in your field first, or you won't be taken seriously.

Dave: How do I accomplish that?

Alex: Begin by delineating your niches.

So that's how I came up with a niche-tiered pyramid. What are niche tiers? Take a peek at mine:

Fortuitously, not too long before my *aha* moment with Alex, Jon and I had had a con-

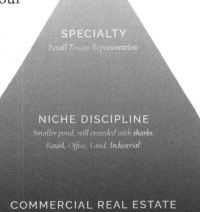

SPECIALTY
Retail Tenant Representation.

NICHE DISCIPLINE
Smaller pond, still crowded with sharks.
Retail, Office, Land, Industrial.

COMMERCIAL REAL ESTATE
Crowded with competition. Noisy. Chasing same opportunities.

versation about niche specialization. Jon enjoyed great relationships with the shopping center owners that our company, Archon, represented, but he wanted to focus on helping tenants and businesses find retail locations. In CRE, we call this "specialized tenant representation," or "tenant rep."

Thanks to Jon's decision to drill down, taken together with his commitment to defining niches within LinkedIn®, he began to execute on tactical initiatives. Jon rolled out 30+ Jersey Mike's Subs locations, leading to master brokerage for a well-known medical brand statewide and nationwide representation for Huey Magoo's Chicken Tenders. All positive disruptors in his quiver.

Jon has executed on major initiatives that are ongoing and clandestine. We only share what we want the public to see. *Moshi moshi* to the *metsubishi* stratagem.

> (Quick Japanese lesson: 目潰し, lit. "eye closers," were tools and techniques that samurai police and others used in feudal Japan to blind or disorient an opponent.)

Further *ninjutsu* quiver tactics involving smoke, mirrors and backchannels will be unveiled in a coming section. Distract and entrance, non-proprietarily, while delivering katana strikes through stealth action. As you perform your enchantments, incrementally pursue secret initiatives designed to take clients or key chess pieces of competitive organizations. Always keep advancing in both modes. Openly clandestine.

Tactical Example

Make your competition think you are a wannabe author, blogger or news personality while you gnaw away at the fruit they never knew was hanging right there for the taking.

Penetrate and entrench future key relationship circles. Create a credibility bulwark as your inter-relational prophylactic. You are already light-years ahead of the digital commoners: You're a Jetson and your clients won't take competitive solicitations seriously. Especially if the competitors lack a digital presence.

Our clients at Archon always fill us in on new solicitations, which we invariably dismiss as amateur. We typically get a good guffaw over the limp attempts and note the rare legit ones, then take aim at the solicitor's contacts if their database is worth it. It's usually not. The real pros only pick battles they have a reasonable chance of winning.

Use cloaked emissaries for further shadow protection and to gain inside-circle intel for full-on offense. Find the centers of gravity that hold your opponents together, go after their best relationships and take their spoils, unapologetically. They started the tussle! Or walk if the intel is unappetizing, which is often the case. You can even refer time-wasting carcass accounts their way. In-depth, cunning and aggressively artful relationship building is forthcoming. Stay tuned.

Cobb Rant: Outside of competitive business, taking sucks and giving rules! Later we will address giving back, which will be my opportunity to deploy a few high-level thank you's via initiatives, not notes. *Tactical LinkedIn® Secrets Give Back,* our advocacy bonus section, is my first enhanced forum to help people through superconnecting. For my money, the best way to thank those who have taught us along the way is to pay it forward: Give to education, instill humility through athletics, mentor and feed our collective communities.

Jon Hellein's tenant representation business is blowing up, and it stands to land many more dragons. I believe fate and execution fused because he was passionately specialized. No doubt his niche specialization will continue to reap rich rewards.

Satisfaction & Rational Passions

Jon packs a vast amount of knowledge in his dealings with the franchise, regional, and national credit brands. He has framed his LinkedIn® content through a B2B real estate prism.

Once Jon, a self-proclaimed "Real Estate Nerd", started sharing insights, our digital community flocked to his content. Blending the rational activities of commercial real estate and tenant representation with content creation, he ultimately spun a string of bankable ideas. The ideas were packaged into smash hit posts with titles such as *12 Practical Tips to Boost Your Tenant Rep Process, Lessons for Young Professionals,* and, last but not least his viral bomb *A Tenant's Guide to Rent Relief.*

Though he may not have realized it, Jon became a genuine "creative," definitely no longer a static consumer. Most importantly, he laid down a foundation for success. The creative-rational process he brought to his article epitomized a fusion of real-world concerns and imaginative packaging—the perfect combo for turning fickle audiences into loyal followers.

Readiness to Strike Relational Targets

Jon's gains are due to meticulous strategic planning for his personal digital brand. He was my inspiration for the earlier Personal Digital Reputation (PDR) section of *Tactical LinkedIn® Secrets*.

For a refresher, a user's PDR is the online footprint created by all of what they say and do on the internet and by what others post about them.

Execution never occurs without a solid base. My personal trainer and confidant, former Pro MMA fighter Jose Figueroa, never landed a knockout punch without solid footing. I bring up Jose because he's my humility-checker, tactical challenger and mental combatant. The first day I trained, he said that I train like an animal. I strive to be that animal in all endeavors. Jose not only challenges me physically. He challenges me psychologically. I pad up and fight him on both fronts.

Jose is a lion in the MMA cage, and paradoxically a lamb of a father. He extends his gloves as a mentor—to many, including me. He teaches that solid footing and fundamentals lead to victory. Train like an animal and prepare diligently for the upcoming digital cage match.

The new B2B octagon is LinkedIn®. What is Jose to Jon in our tactical maneuvers? Jon is now a young lion and ready to hunt digitally. Focused preparation is key to execution and he's Jonny-on-the-spot.

If you visit Jon's profile you'll see:

> Jon did a phenomenal job of showcasing his last three engagement arrows striking the target and drawing positive attention. His two posts received more than 208 engagements, 98 comments and 55 thousand plus views.

Jon's first article, *12 Practical Tips to Boost Your Tenant Rep Process*, received 499 deep views, 74 engagements and 16 comments on a deep read. That's a whopping 15 percent engagement rate, where a strong post gets 2 percent to 4 percent.

> Interaction with Industry Leaders & Influencers—The word "influencer" is now overused, bouge or cliché, depending on the audience. Whatever the rap, influence is the goal, and relationship building with powerful decision makers is the path to success.

Jon, Janet and I sat down to discuss specialization on LinkedIn® and discovered we had material for an ongoing series. We were no longer linked out. We purchased LinkedIn® Premium and created a path to prowess. There was no end to our enthusiasm. We just needed to figure out what was going to work.

TOPIC 3:

SHOOT, MISS & DELETE = DIGITAL LEARNING CURVES

I n LinkedIn® and in life, there's a learning curve. Approach this curve slowly and cautiously because a lot of people want to see you drive off a cliff. That typically won't happen unless you do something very thoughtless, malicious or hotheaded. Approach LinkedIn® methodically and passionately regarding your content, but dispassionately about things you cannot control.

Posts can get thousands of views and a range of good and bad comments. Negative commentary is more common in other social media spaces because LinkedIn® is professional, career oriented and it polices their members. Recall that LinkedIn® is a business too, aiming to benefit you.

Cobb Rant: Keep in mind though, that trolls lurk in the digisphere, and they may engage with you on LinkedIn®. Stay level-headed and don't get pulled into their games. There's no dearth of ding-dongs who are out to invade your feed, swipe your business, tarnish your rep. Take the higher road, the right road, and your current and prospective clients will take note. That speaks volumes of your company character and culture. Delete the ding-dong (my synonym for dumbass), and dilemma solved.

Don't fret, shake or shiver. Instead, add some arrows to your digital quiver. We'll teach you to dispose of comments with the efficiency of a politician mired in scandal and block your detractors like NFL great William "The Fridge" Perry! Your LinkedIn® feed is your digital endzone. Protect it.

Every organization, industry or situation is different, but LinkedIn® is the common incubator. Grow your presence strategically and thoughtfully without regard for the bullies who may berate you, flamers or troubadours of stupidity who may try to bait you.

Always remember, you have a moat and arrows. You are empowered to defend your realm and mute any encroaching barbarians from the land of Ding-dong. Delete uncivil or inflammatory comments. Block the ding-dong if the problem persists. Publicly cutting down brutishness, especially if satire is combined with cunning, can create an emotional war bond with your reader.

Then, sometimes, your content may just be okay. And that's okay too.

Rebounding from Missed Shots

Do you remember the first time you swung a golf club, shot a basketball, attempted Brazilian Jiu-Jitsu or tried competitive Canadian curling? I bet you weren't Tiger Woods, Michael Jordan, Royce Gracie or Kevin Martin aka "K-Mart" on the ice your first time.

Winners miss but do not lament. They keep playing because the final score is what ultimately matters. Some of the most insightful, well-thought-out, compelling and profound content falls like silent redwoods on deaf ears. Conversely, some of the most imbecilic, uninformed and downright weird posts can explode on everyone's feed to viral applause.

Abnormality = Virality

Viral Halloween Costume

➢ Views: 35,676
➢ Likes: 374
➢ Hover Emojis: 75
➢ Comments: 38

103 Year Old Lady Celebrates Surviving Coronavirus with a Bud Light

➢ Views: 50,492
➢ Likes: 1,235
➢ Hover Emojis: 190
➢ Comments: 104

Viral is cool, but it doesn't really matter in the long run. Want to know what does? Your PDR history! And now want to know the good news? Timeless and quality posts purge inconsequential, boring and obtuse content. Vlogs, blogs and longform posts feed the algorithm, and the digital world perpetually turns on LinkedIn® in everyone's collective feed.

Flood Away Duds

Once you post content, it's in your history unless you delete it. People can search your LinkedIn® history back to the beginning. That's all fine and good, but the typical person has the attention span of a gnat. Unless an operative is performing a deep dive, most digital divers are not industrious enough to effectively investigate and notate. The typical searcher will look back at five to 10 posts.

Your goal as a content creator should be similar to that of a golfer's handicap. Strive to make 10 of your last 20 posts strong, dynamic and helpful to your audience. Deliver utility for their quiver. Ty Cobb hit the ball one out of every three times in (.367 batting average), and Babe Ruth hit home runs around every 11 at bats. That doesn't matter, no game, including high-level relationship building, will go smoothly every play.

Look at your LinkedIn® year like a head coach would approach a professional sports season:

DIGITAL QUIVER
SCOUT AND ADAPT

Content Distribution Initiatives
- ➢ Figure out the content schedule. Predetermine times to drop bombs.
- ➢ Scout the competition and "watch film." In other words, research what plays work for the other team.
- ➢ Halftime adjustments. Learn from mistakes, adjust to the game, implement and counterbalance your opponent's strategy.
- ➢ Execute on your strengths, impel digital muscle memory and repeat.
- ➢ Dominate through good content and strategic interactions.

TOPIC 4:

BOOM, I'M HERE!

CAPITALIZE ON DESIRED OUTCOMES

You are posting and people are noticing. You've arrived in Hollywood, but there's still no paparazzi. Fifteen minutes of fame last about that long on LinkedIn®. A post is a snapshot. Your feed is fleeting and may vanish into obscurity. After all, we are a "What-have-you-done-for-me-lately?" society that lazily yearns for instant gratification and Instagramification. Do not get delusions of grandeur. The public's memory is transitory. But if you fix their problems with your ideas, your targets will respond appreciatively and meld into your thought influence repository.

Once you create the desired outcome in business, record, deploy and recycle. Great content is similar to a classic book or song. Timeless, passable and re-salvageable. It's a matter of calibrated dynamic content. Repurpose your content and fire away again. Success breeds success and relationships.

KEYS TO EXECUTION

LinkedIn® is the most cost-effective marketing tool for under-dogs to showcase accomplishments and success stories against larger Goliaths. Tilt your bow upward, aim and release arrows to disrupt conventions, shift paradigms and shatter glass ceilings and relational webs. The next tier of relationship building...

TOPIC 5:

TIER YOUR PYRAMIDS

TERRACE UPWARD

I t's game time and you're scoring content on LinkedIn®. Engagement, statistics and your online presence are on the uptick. Congrats, your legend develops! Hardly the moment to rest on your laurels. Each new round lets you build on your momentum. Gear up, tier up and keep sparring in better sandboxes. Now let's go take some relational toys...

Tiers, Tears & Tears

Tear up the old playbook: Don't shed a tear about your rookie online presence and let's capture relationships a few tiers higher, equaling more success and money. Smartest person in the room? Never. Nor the know-it-all who doesn't play well or learn well.

Be open-minded yet discerning—rather than confirming bias-bantering blatherskites.

Deploy touch arrows upward to grow onward. Approach your digital relationships as if your professional life depended on it. In a certain sense it does. These relationships can change your life. The goal is to be invited to the grownups' table at a noisy, bustling Thanksgiving dinner even though yams are awful and so are the Lions.

Cobb Rant: Excuse yourself from the kiddies and pull up a chair with the digital adults, where the real cornucopia of opportunities exists. And please don't talk politics around the turkey. Elephants and donkeys can cause damage to your personal digital résumé.

Aim high and up your circle of influence. How? Once again, preparation is key, and we created a map to snaring secrets. The tactical niche pyramid.

Digital LinkedIn® Quiver
➢ Create a niche pyramid for your career and terrace to specialization.
➢ Terrace a separate pyramid for LinkedIn® content.
➢ Once the subspecialties are established, deploy digital touch arrows (InMail, comments, emojis).
➢ Design content specifically directed at tiered targets.

The niche pyramid will be your map to the aforementioned cliché and bourgeois word: influencers. Those who don't invite everyone. Not only can they influence your work life, but also your well-being. We are social animals and other people influence our health and happiness, whether professional, personal, or intimate.

Navigate the digital social landscape through niche pathways and you will succeed. With some help from your strategically targeted friends and executed relationships.

Me? I get by with a little help from my friends too. Take Jon, one of my best. I was his mentor. Through time and scars, reciprocity blossomed in mentorship. Below is his story, real-time and in living color.

TACTICAL APPLICATION:
JON HELLEIN'S BINARY JOURNEY_

Looking back on our pixelated journey, Jon was befuddled by my initial article, which was part of an overarching content strategy release. My first articles addressed cannabis, and my biggest writing inspiration is Robert *"The 48 Laws of Power"* Greene. Combining Machiavellian strategies with Cheech Marin right off the bat raised Jon's eyebrows. Over a few hard-hitting, emphatic and cantankerous debates, Jon shared his concerns:

1. "Would this exposure detrimentally affect the cultivation of current and future key relationships?"
2. "Will they (referring to the B2B and CRE communities) have verbal and written ammunition to use against us?"
3. "How does a cannabis article on LinkedIn® advance Archon's commercial real estate business?

My answers are:
1. I hope not, but **** happens.
2. Maybe.
3. Writing about cannabis from a broad, land use perspective allows us to engage the B2B community's non-proprietary attention while Archon is executing on back-channel, pro-

prietary market initiatives. It's also a controversial topic that large, encumbered organizations cannot address—due to an assortment of red-tape tripwires.

> "In today's business and political climate, there is no other industry that better epitomizes the interweaving of relevance and controversy than medical marijuana." –DAVID COBB AKA COBBY AKA SNOOP COBBY COBB*

Candor, Resolution & Collective Realizations

As Archon's publishing platform Linked into our digital community, digitally and deal-wise, the compliments from real estate experts, trusted advisors and respected colleagues exploded. The compliments were the elephant on the seesaw, and the criticisms were the mouse. We had the guts to broach a controversial, yet hot and relevant topic at the time. Our thoroughness was immensely appreciated.

I was relieved. I can't think of one relationship my writing damaged, and Jon's author journey started shortly thereafter. Jon and Janet's support was my pillar. It still is.

A <u>Real</u> Real Estate Conversation About LinkedIn®

David Cobb (from across office): Hey man, we're getting some good company publicity from these blogs. I think it would be really good for your CRE brand. Industry leaders and experts are reading mine. Would you want to write one? I'll help.

Jon Hellein: NAHHHH.

Cobb: Come on, dude, it will really help get your name out there as a Tenant Rep Specialist. What if I wrote an outline for you?
Jon: Nope.

Cobb: You are such an idiot. Come on! You like sharing knowledge and mentoring the youngins in commercial real estate. All you need to do is fill in the outline.

Jon: You're right. I still don't know. Maybe I'll think about it.

Cobb: Cool. (Internal monologue: Boom!)

The Camel's Nose Outline

I got my nose in the tent, and the camel (that would be shortform writing) soon nudged Jon over the hump of ambivalence. I lost no time in banging out an outline. From there I knew I could hook him into hanging flesh on the bones. I could get him across the virtual Sahara. After all, we were sharing expert advice for our community. The topic was our best tips for representing dynamic businesses, and I knew the content would be well received.

I needed one more Royce Gracie armbar to jiu-jitsu Jon into authorship submission. (Royce Gracie, by the way, gained fame for his success in the Ultimate Fighting Championship. I like a good fight! And a hard-fought win.)

"Just Go"—Make Some Noise! = Dave Cobb (to Jon Hellein)

Back when Jon and I were both younger and less emotionally intelligent, he would come to me pretty much every time he hit a fork in the road. Very early in his career, I told him, "Just go"

There aren't many things if you screw up (different word at the time) that I can't fix."

Building on my outline, Jon compounded subheadings and wrote an amazing first draft. He was tactically prepared. Even excited. We huddled on some editorial lifts and polished that diamond to bling-bling.

His first article *12 Tips to Boost Your Tenant Rep Process* glistened to thundering applause from allies and competitors. Check out stats and hoops metrics at the end of the section. Many moons later, with the COVID-19 shutdown, tenants needed advice. Perilously and desperately. Jon had the insight and tactical expertise to swoop in and help, via LinkedIn® and discussed in detail. To come.

Waterfall Mentorship

Not many people know this, but Jon's team was the inaugural winner of the annual UCF NAIOP Case Study competition in 2009. Fast forward more than a decade and Jon and Janet are now sharing their knowledge as mentors for the current case competition. The students aced their Zoom-based presentation in the early days of the coronavirus outbreak.

> Cooler news, the Archon team pulled through with a "W," making Jon the only undefeated student and mentor within the esteemed history of the competition! #realestatedorkbada**.

Following the presentation, Jon and the Archon team produced a short video for all the kids in the presentation. It was a win-win. Archon got a morale boost from the teamwork and kind deed. And the kids felt valued both by our exertions and our results.

Jon actually has no idea I filmed this video. I was pretending like I was texting, because he hates videos. The first time he will see it is when the book is published. What's he gonna do? Sue me? I'm his partner…probably for life…

If, and only if, it's sincere, tactically giving back can be the most efficient arrow to disarm decision makers and nurture long-term relationships. Only aim for immediate reciprocity and your relational arrow has zero velocity. Quiver-arm to disarm and become a Quiver-Giver!

Viral Advice & Duress Relief

At the beginning of the coronavirus shutdown, Jon came to me with an idea to craft a manual or guide for our key relationships. Many of our tenant representation clients and friends approached Jon, Janet and me for advice. These are small business owners with employees, franchisees with families and business people with accountability. He was having the same repetitive conversation over and over.

He pensively and deliberately set aside time and thought about arming our clients, allies and colleagues' quivers for negotiation. The world was bottoming out. The crisis could financially and figuratively infect our clients' livelihood as well as those of their families and employees. Jon created a draft, Janet and I provided some insight and Jon pulled the trigger. Ultimately triggering a barrage of reciprocal goodwill.

The payoff of *Tenant's Guide to Rent Relief* was phenomenal. Beyond the online engagement, our organization was inundated with requests for the sharable PDF. You can't download sharable PDFs from LinkedIn® Documents. That was by design. Emails are the new gold rush. We corralled influencers our way and made some phenomenal new contacts during those weeks. Want to know why Jon hit paydirt? He used tactics to fix problems. Period.

Followers: 10X INCREASE: 10,313—Started at under 1,000

12 Practical Tips to Boost Your Tenant Rep Process:

➢ 499 Views
➢ 74 Likes
➢ 5 Hover Emojis
➢ 16 Comments
➢ 5 Shares

Tenant's Guide to Rent Relief:

➢ 32,465 Views
➢ 184 Likes
➢ 15 Hover Emojis
➢ 55 Comments
➢ 29 Reshares

> "When I first started on LinkedIn®, I watched a lot of Gary Vaynerchuk (Gary V), and my two major takeaways were: Be first, and ii) add value by giving." **–JON HELLEIN**

KEYS TO EXECUTION

If your content panders to the masses, no one will receive your message clearly. Find successful alcoves of the influential and touch them emphatically and empathically. Nearly every successful expert on LinkedIn® niche-specializes to connect with their audience. How should you connect with your audience?

The simple steps come from an inward-facing and generous frame of mind. Don't ration your passion. Share your knowledge. And above all, don't be fake. Authenticity and specialized problem solving are a key tactical secret to your success.

Jon Hellein showed his authentic self to an audience, initiated a content creation program and grew a specialized following. This led to new relationships, inside-market intel, off-market deal opportunities and multiple invites to the big table. Jon's LinkedIn® initiatives and high-level networking have translated into seven-figure returns of newly generated revenue for the Archon organization.

As a reasonably young, cost-conscious and growth-focused organization, we cannot imagine a better ROI for hundreds of dollars per year, leading to millions in returns over time. But, and there's always a "but," when something sounds too good to be true... Right?

> **Cobb Rant:** Pull your head out of it. The inevitable pain in the butt is that you have to invest time to get returns over time. Endure and grow in a calibrated tactical manner. Let's learn some manners: how to behave in the real world of creative content and production. Read on for an etiquette lesson that no amount of flashy money can buy.

It's time to gear up and tier up again, with calibrated dynamic content. Speaking of which, the next section will spotlight three dynamic women and their prowess in creating dynamic content that's carefully aligned with needs and strategic goals.

You have just added to your digital quiver with:

➢ **Digital Perception Is Reality**: Pivot, Brand-Build & Establish Prominence
➢ **Targeted Niches & Brand Differentiation**

Next up in *Tactical LinkedIn® Secrets* is **Section 5**, in which you will learn:

➢ **Calibrated Dynamic Content**: Authenticity, Vulnerability & Mass Connectivity with High-Level Digital Allies

➢ **Control of Public Narrative by Executing in the Shadows**: Digital Ninja Weapons

CALIBRATED DYNAMIC CONTENT

AUTHENTICITY, VULNERABILITY & MASS CONNECTIVITY—WITH HIGH-LEVEL DIGITAL ALLIES

"I don't give a **** what anybody thinks, when you're a racehorse, the reason they put blinders on these things is because if you look at the horse on the left or the right, [they're] going to miss a step. That's why the horses have blinders on. And that's what people should have. When you're running after something, you should not look left or right—what does this person think, what does that person think? No. Go."
–Jimmy Iovine, legendary record producer

Y ou pulled off a niche pivot to success, through expert, focused and dynamic content creation. Now it's time to unlock a secret process I call Creative Blinders.

Just as racehorses have zero chance of winning without blinders, also called blinkers, to keep them on track, don't bet on digital freewheeling to gain a competitive edge on LinkedIn®. The odds are appalling.

Let's create a photo finish worthy of Churchill Downs Racetrack through dynamic content. Tactical, deliberate and calibrated for maximum problem solving and knowledge building. First step: We'll add blinders to your digital quiver so you can ignore wayward distractions and keep your eyes on the prize. Your horse will win.

TOPIC 1:

GAIN KNOWLEDGE, POST INSIGHTS, ACHIEVE INFLUENCE

C reating content is no time to freak out or lament. If you want to build your brand and business, you have to be known. That means you have to let go of the fear and ego and let it rip.

Freak? Lament? See if any of these lame lamentation scenarios sound familiar:

- ➤ LAMENT: I don't have access to video production.
  - o Anti-Lament: There's an invention on your phone called a camera. Use it.
- ➤ LAMENT: I have writer's block.
  - o Anti-Lament: Create a detailed outline and start writing words. Deadlines kill writer's block. Don't freak out, Superfreak! Consider yourself the digital Rick James now, a multi-instrumentalist and producer. "Just go" create accountability through hard timelines.

> ➢ LAMENT: I don't know where to start. (Here we go, writer's block again.)
>> o Anti-Lament: Ask a good writer for help. Get by with a little help.

Thirty years ago, no one had access to digital channels except for the elite, the media and the military who created it. That paradigm disintegrated along with boy bands and Barney (thankfully, and a shout out to David Wolf at Audivita.com). As forward-thinking business people, we've collectively run out of excuses for not having an online presence. By presence, I mean you must post. In cadence.*

*You don't see the capital "C" here, but as the adoring father of a Cadence, I do.

How to do so can be learned, within LinkedIn®. But you can't bring weak vanilla garbage to the LinkedIn® basket or it will get Mutumbo'd* into the stands. What's the equivalent of getting your shiznit swatted by a 7'2" Congolese Naismith Hall of Famer? Engagement crickets. It fouls your creative floating, especially when significant practice was put in. Once again, LinkedIn® embodies the interconnectivity of knowledge and creativity.

*In case you don't know whom I was referencing: Dikembe Mutombo Mpolondo Mukamba Jean-Jacques Wamutombo. #coolestnameever #NoNoNo https://en.wikipedia.org/wiki/Dikembe_Mutombo

Cobb Rant: Sales tactics, social selling, promotional videos, blogs, recruiting and job search are the quintessential words associated with LinkedIn®. That's how it began, but those who still view it that way should request a VHS version of this book.

Here's a 21ˢᵗ-century update: LinkedIn® is a creative platform fueled by creatives. Everyone's content can be fodder to fortify your brand. Research and harvest. And while you're at it, plant your own seeds. This is where it gets fun and where you can let your creativity run.

Till the field.

> "Build it and they will come." **–RAY KINSELLA,** *FIELD OF DREAMS*

For analytical types, LinkedIn® offers acres of information to engage the left brain. But in today's amber waves, it's the creative right brainers who reap and sow the field. Dreamers. Especially if management-creatives.

Creatives have produced instructional videos, hosted live events with leaders, written real-time articles and have kept us engaged, without bias, on LinkedIn®. This professional platform is a relatively neutral beacon amongst an unremitting fog of demagogues.

> "We know what we are, but not what we may be."
> **–WILLIAM SHAKESPEARE**

Run the LinkedIn® rabbit hole and guess what you'll find? More rabbit holes, or what I call serendipitous side shoots. You never know where they will take you. Any connection can have a robust and prosperous result. It may, at times, be serendipitous when you land on just the right person to help or serve. Often, it's because you put the effort in to communicating and offering value, within LinkedIn®.

As covered previously, the first step to sprouting nutritious content is to begin reading and identifying reliable information sources. Want interesting content? Do something interesting for your following. Inform and alleviate problems!

Cobb Rant: Citing crackpots is an easy way to tarnish your PDR and look lazy. Carefully vet your references and common connections and scrutinize their PDRs.

The below reflect some phenomenal LinkedIn® content and relationship mines:
- ➢ Amazon (18,778,832 followers)
- ➢ LinkedIn® (15,382,061 followers)
- ➢ Microsoft (13,904,586 followers)
- ➢ Ted Talks (1,504,062 followers)
- ➢ *The New York Times* (6,153,871 followers)
- ➢ Fox News Media *(222,041 followers)*
- ➢ CNN (2,849,583 followers)
- ➢ Deloitte (6,780,191 followers)
- ➢ *The Wall Street Journal* (8,633,653 followers)
- ➢ *The Washington Post* (1,467,630 followers)
- ➢ National Geographic (3,201,678 followers)
- ➢ McKinsey & Company (3,849,201 followers)
- ➢ Yale University (297,478 followers)

➢ DePauw University (25,920 followers)
➢ Crummer Graduate School of Business (7,897 followers)

LinkedIn® people & influencers:
➢ Ryan Roslansky, CEO at LinkedIn® (338,282 Followers)
➢ Jeff Weiner, Executive Chairman, Former CEO, LinkedIn® (10,767,660 followers). Weiner's actually dropped by around 100k and Roslansky's more than doubled since the fall of 2020.
➢ Bill Gates, Co-chair, Bill & Melinda Gates Foundation (32,229,561 followers)
➢ Tony Robbins, #1 *New York Times* bestselling author; life and business strategist; philanthropist; entrepreneur (6,459,511 followers)
➢ Melinda Gates, Co-chair, Bill & Melinda Gates Foundation; Founder, Pivotal Ventures; author, *The Moment of Lift.* (6,081,740 followers)
➢ Barbara Corcoran, Founder, The Corcoran Group; Shark, ABC's *Shark Tank*; public speaker; podcast host; author (1,185,050 followers)
➢ Oprah Winfrey, Chairman & CEO, Harpo Productions; producer; publisher; actress; innovator (995,757 followers)
➢ Tim Tebow, Heisman Trophy winner; 3x *New York Times* bestselling author; college football analyst (1,050,351 followers)
➢ Suze Orman, Founder, Suze Orman Financial Group, personal finance expert (536,318 followers)
➢ Daniel Roth, Editor in Chief, LinkedIn® News (309,325 followers)

> ➤ Pau Gasol, professional athlete; President, Gasol Foundation; Official Candidate, International Olympic Committee Athletes Commission (75,263 followers)
> ➤ Mark Cuban (without trying: 6,586,961)
> ➤ Jordyn Dahl (Entrepreneurship Editor at LinkedIn® News (47,650 followers)

Who are your influencers? List them and get to know them.

> "Your presence on LinkedIn® and online in general, or lack thereof, will positively or detrimentally affect your maneuverability in life, business and your ability to give back to your specific community. Specialized, thought provoking and problem-solving content is key. Especially advocacy."
> —**RAAMEL MITCHELL**, DIRECTOR, MICROSOFT CITIZENSHIP AND MARKET DEVELOPMENT

These business leaders, thought leaders, and cause-advocacy leaders are the tip of the iceberg concerning the amount of knowledge and connectivity you can ingress and access.

Note: The above stats are current as I write. Not for long, of course, or as George Carlin put it, *"Just when I discovered the meaning of life, they changed it."* But speaking of stats, let's take time out for a little numbers dance: A whopping 95 percent of B2B content marketers go with LinkedIn® for their organic content marketing, and 88 percent of the platform's top performing B2B content marketers prioritize their audience's info needs over their own.

Wait, there's more. Some 90 million of LinkedIn®'s users are high-level influencers, and 63 million of them occupy decision making positions. Consider this math an encouraging kick in the pants to step up your dynamic content and multiply the big figures in your world.

A thank you to LinkedIn® editors: I want to give a shout out to the LinkedIn® editors, specifically Editor in Chief, Daniel Roth and Entrepreneurship Editor Jordyn Dahl. Both were a trove of critical insight during virulent times. For daily quick reads that directly affect the business community, check out these thinkers and doers on the LinkedIn® editorial team whose coverage is instrumental to staying tactically current and are some of my favorite sources: Alexander Besant, Callie Schweitzer, Andrew Seaman and Kelli Nguyen.

 DIGITAL QUIVER:
CONTENT ACCESS POINTS & INTERNAL RESOURCES

➢ LinkedIn® Publishing: Add Images & Rich Media

➢ Use the new Newsletter Feature: How to Start a Newsletter

➢ Best Practices:

➢ Search people and organizations
➢ Reference the LinkedIn® news feed

Connect with your audience as a creator through avid research and dynamic video production and writing. We will arm your rich-media and verbal quiver while also adding digital chainmail for your reputational protection. The naked emperor syndrome is damaging and, luckily, very avoidable.

THE NAKED EMPEROR

(REAL VS. IDEALIZED SELF)

"The Emperor shivered, for he suspected they were right. But he thought, 'This procession has got to go on.' So he walked more proudly than ever, as his noblemen held high the train that wasn't there at all."
–Excerpt from *The Emperor's Clothes,* **Hans Christian Anderson**

Cobb Rant: Let's start with a digital loincloth. "Fake it till you make it" won't work for long. Naked emperors, charlatans and fake billionaires exist in many forms online and this section will model a self-destructive weapon never to include in your quiver.

The point of this exercise is to illuminate your potential blind spots and preempt any stumbles into the inferno of failed posts. Drawn from real-life flameouts, the samples you'll encounter contain cautionary tales. Some content is just moronic. Forced, self-important, mind numbing and so bad it's like watching *Sharknado*. If you want to disarm your digital quiver and clear a path to failure, begin by creating exceptionally atrocious posts:

Content Forewarnings

> "In fighting and in everyday life, you should be determined through calm. Meet the situation without tenseness yet not recklessly, your spirit settled yet unbiased. An elevated spirit is weak and a low spirit is weak. Do not let the enemy see your spirit." –MIYAMOTO MUSASHI

Keys to Atrociousness

➢ **Narcissism** is a great way to immediately disconnect from your audience and make them revile you. Want negativity? Post a picture of your yacht, sports cars, jewelry, expensive purses or private jet. Brag and your digital brand will lag.

➢ **Inconsequential Content** is an eye-closing strategy that, if implemented to its fullest, will bore the boring out of your following. Nobody wants to see boomerang videos of your brunch mates devouring avocado toast and mimosas for the nth weekend in a row.

➢ **Self-Promotion** is the inbred cousin of narcissism and inconsequential content. Keep braying about what you've done, deals you closed, title-only promotions and updates with no flare. Show a few high-end purchases, horse or

Porsche, and you'll land a me-me knockout to your online brand. You'll become the channel on the TV that only plays commercials. Oops, that channel doesn't exist because no one would watch. Careful of whom you claim to know, whether business moguls, celebrities or a notable in your home court. If they mess up? You're guilty by association. It's nice to promote good works but exercise great caution.

➤ **Political Discussions** are a guaranteed way to alienate half your audience. Imagine the aforementioned Thanksgiving table with Aunt Barbara quoting the opposition leader and yelling at Uncle Frank for wearing his preferred candidate's cap. A tip for your life quiver: Political rants are a waste of time. Ever seen them change anyone's mind? How fitting that the word "political" so echoes "apocalyptic."

Cobb Rant: Best case, half of your cornucopia falls off the table. Worse case, your reputation gets cran-buried, a reputation that instead must be cultivated, enhanced and maintained. Demagogue online and you will get flogged and maligned. Your digital reputation will fly like a turkey and your wishbones will get snapped in the wrong direction.

➤ Realize that people value their time as much as you value yours. Bring value or no one will engage. How do you do that? Imbue authenticity and elicit expertise. Negativity, self-aggrandization, hot air and political prisms will keep you in a state of online-presence attrition. Tactically focus and envision. You now have the digital blinders that will allow you to trot gallantly to the winner's circle.

> "Almost universally, the kind of performance we give on social media is positive. It's more "Let me tell you how well things are going. Look how great I am." It's rarely the truth: "I'm scared. I'm struggling. I don't know." **-RYAN HOLIDAY**, *EGO IS THE ENEMY*

Digital Charlatans, Posers & Fakers Making It!

Don't get me started on disingenuous people. The web has them in spades. You will learn not only to sniff them out, but to deploy their tactics to further your self-interest.

Cobb Rant: Digital charlatans have mass appeal and often use pandering to get it—with catch phrases like "Lead Pipeline Expert," "60 Days to LinkedIn® Success," "We Help Executives Become Content Creators." Don't buy it! It's the LinkedIn® equivalent of junk mail. Marketing ploys.

Vet your prospective contacts carefully, especially their accomplishments and credentials. Fill your quiver with trustworthy relationships and keep it real. Ditch the digital posers.

I will give a little slack to those who "fake it a little" in the beginning. But heed this warning: Your day in court will come. Be judicious in how you represent yourself. The easiest way to circumvent the pitfalls that come with lack of experience is to find a mentor and fortify your credibility. I found an amazing new one while writing this book. Luminescence in the dog-eat-dog darkness. My sockeroo guru, Irv Weinberg, author of *First Dog on Earth* (firstdogbook.com).

So what does it take to make a splash in today's communications deluge? We now have access to infinite information as attention spans paradoxically diminish. Hook your audience with remembrances and bonds, together with your ideas, trend forecasts and industry views—or another fisherman will reel in the big relationship catch.

You will never know the big fish that swam right underneath you. Lash high-level waters with a digital trident:

1. EXPERTISE

2. CREDIBILITY

3. AUTHENTICITY

1. Expertise
2. Credibility
3. Authenticity

The first two are attained; the latter is engrained. My Site Source friends Marti Weinstein, LinkedIn® ally Stacey Mooney and partner Janet Galvin triumph in all three.

TACTICAL APPLICATION:
AUTHENTICITY–JANET GALVIN, CO-FOUNDER, ARCHON COMMERCIAL ADVISORS

Janet was my mentor when I first got into commercial real estate in 2005. She was a digital thoroughbred out of the gate, because authenticity combined with expertise is a winning ticket for building new relationships. In retail commercial real estate, in her lane, with blinders and quiver-rich expertise.

She began with under 1,000 followers at Archon's inception and now has 13,692. For a little perspective, the average CRE principal in Florida hovers at around 2,500.

Janet's recent successes have mapped with her growing presence as a LinkedIn® blogger and vlogger who delivers value to her audience in the form of authentic, useful, sharable conversation sparks. Take for example her blog post titled "Best Practices for Uncertain Times." It featured this relatable quote under the subheading *Differentiate Through Honesty*:

Janet told me she thought it was "amazing that [I'm] willing to share all this knowledge that is really gonna help everyone, even our friendly competitors." Okay, *entre nous*, Janet had a little help here. We collaborated on an outline. She wrote a draft. I added content and gave an editorial lift. We published on her LinkedIn®. We raised a toast. A handful of hours produced a dynamic, informative and recyclable asset. Partnered or outsourced, this sort of marketing resource is a quiver-create away. Draw your bowstring and release.

Be authentic and the rest will flow. Boors and braggards will inevitably traverse rough waters. Is your content seaworthy? Inauthentic flotsam sinks low, only to be consumed by bottom feeders. Credibility is your buoy.

> "I now use LinkedIn® much more than ever in the past. These days it's my bible to see what's going on." **–JANET GALVIN** (VETERAN CRE DEALMAKER)

TACTICAL APPLICATION:
CREDIBILITY–MARTI WEINSTEIN, ASSOCIATE, ZELL COMMERCIAL

She's one of my favorite young ninjas. We first met Marti Weinstein in Section 1, and now let's check in with the 20-something commercial real estate professional, about establishing cred on LinkedIn®.

Marti draws a bead on the importance of cultivating trust and adding value through her much-shared videos that bolster her PDR. Unlike a "For Lease, Call This Number" sign at a shopping center, "sharing a video of a listing with all of the users you're trying to target in that trade area" enables a more personal, ongoing connection. Which is why Marti makes sure "to post meaningful content" every time.

"That always turns into a direct message," she reports. From invitations to meet up at the annual ICSC (International Council of Shopping Centers) conference to simply, "You're in my market? Let's grab coffee!" Marti has unlocked "a lot of relationship building through posting meaningful content on LinkedIn®." As she notes, it's the only "platform out there that can allow for those authentic conversations without having to buy a list of phone numbers or go through some of the old-school tactics of getting in touch with people."

Marti continues, "So as much as I want to build more exposure and be on the forefront of my network's mind, I want to do that in a way that reflects how I operate in my business and how I want to be perceived in the market."

Marti as a rookie started with followers in the hundreds and has grown organically to 5,119 in the span of a year. Her follower count is catching fire and growing exponentially through her posting and video efforts.

> "I want my landlord clients who follow me on LinkedIn® to be proud that I represent their assets and not look at me like, What kind of image is she projecting?!"
>
> **–MARTI WEINSTEIN,** UP-AND-COMING CRE NINJA

TACTICAL APPLICATION:
RESOLVE–STACEY MOONEY, CRE MATCHMAKER, FOUNDER/CEO, RETAIL LIVE!

Janet and Stacey have each established themselves as experts in commercial real estate with enviable track records as proof. What brought them to the next level were the X-factors we mentioned above. Being real is the most crucial arrow in your quiver! I can think of few better examples than the heart pouring Stacey shared as the pandemic hit.

"On March 13th, I fought through a lot of tears and made the toughest business decision of my life." So starts the LinkedIn® article Stacey wrote about cancelling her ninth annual Retail Live!, a networking and dealmaking bash that COVID-19 was now bashing. Titled *"How to Win When You Are Losing It All,"* the article hooked readers right away with a relatable dilemma and quickly brought them into the soft underbelly of Stacey's logistical, professional, financial and emotional ordeal.

Fearing for the future of her brand, she wondered, "Would Retail Live! survive or would it slip into oblivion like so many retailers who will never reopen?" The stakes were especially high for this single mother facing a significant hit, both from revenue loss and from the convention hotel bill she was in the hock for.

But far from a tale of woe, *How to Win* offered a redemptive arc worthy of a Hollywood classic: "Even during all of the fear, I had a nagging voice that there was an opportunity in the midst of this crisis," she shared, withholding tears.

Next the reader learned about her inspired idea to make the show's trade book available as a free download, along with two previous editions. Stacey's generosity not only let would-be Retail Live! attendees access site criteria, exhibitors' contact info and sponsor ads, but it meant that her team's "blood, sweat and tears would [not] go down the drain." She reflected, "It felt awesome to take the focus off of my problems, utilize a wealth of knowledge/contacts and help others."

Talk about silver linings. "Strangers called to say thank you and expressed gratitude for my 'no strings' attitude," she wrote, adding, "Our team is stronger, I've grown personally, and our brand will evolve to better suit our customer's needs. I have forged new friendships with people who were merely acquaintances before the pandemic. We have bonded over the difficult choices, experienced collective loss, and are allies in the new theater of business."

For the kicker, Stacey updated the article with the newsflash that the international hotel chain released Retail Live! from their contractual obligations. Further reasons to celebrate: She has parlayed part of the trade show into a successful webinar series called *"Meet the Retailers."*

Staying genuine and letting down her guard allowed Stacey to tell her story via this post and a linked companion video. She told it in a way that thrummed a resonant chord with her target audience. I was honored to give her first draft an editorial lift and can't agree more with her takeaway: to help selflessly, offer assistance to those in hard times, show vulnerability and radiate a positive voice. That is when you will experience personal and non-monetary wealth. I was gratified to see that my initial advice suggesting that Stacey write a reflective article about a time that was transitional, transformational, and transcending paid off handsomely. To this day.

Janet and Stacey are both #CRE influencers with over 13,155 and 13,692 followers respectively. I bet you're thinking "Followers, so what Dave, I want to make money." I will emphasize that if you stay cyclically connected to influencers your endeavors will inevitably monetize. Janet and Stacey are currently working a massive fitness deal and I closed a multi-million dollar deal with Stacey a few years ago—lucrative interconnectivity.

> "LinkedIn® is the greenhouse where game changing relationships and repetitive and novel deal making is cultivated."
> **–STACEY MOONEY** (CRE ENTREPRENEUR)

TOPIC 3:

THE CONTENT QUIVER

READ ON TO BE FULLY ARMED

> "A picture is worth 1,000 words. A video is worth 1,000 pictures." **–MOI, (COBB)** AUTHOR OF *TACTICAL LINKEDIN® SECRETS*

This may be the only time I ever get quoted in a book, so I'm taking advantage of that "shiznit," a term coined by one my favorite wordsmiths (arrow) Calvin Broadus, Jr. aka Snoop Dogg.

Early '90s gangsta rap jokes aside, I couldn't think of a more applicable quote than the aforementioned. LinkedIn® is accelerating sensory experiences. Please don't lick your computer screen!

LinkedIn®: In the Beginning

> ➤ Static imagery and documents in résumés, job postings, business cards, etc.

LinkedIn®: Fast Forward

> ➤ Digitization of humanization with rich-media options—visual, audio and interactive for:
>   - o Pictures
>   - o Articles
>   - o Newsletters
>   - o Documents (included no keyword function)
>   - o Podcasts
>   - o Videos

The Gradation of Content Creation

You've glimpsed the LinkedIn® content arsenal. But how battle ready are you? Read on for Tactical LinkedIn® Secrets to creative dominance.

Pictures: Click Picking & Timestamping

A picture will enmesh your networks. They grant instantaneous interconnectivity. How is that? Tag, you're it. Get chasing and tagging. Remember to take pictures whenever in the company of established LinkedIn® users and leading personalities. Tag your posts identifying whom you're with and watch them go viral. Clicking, uploading and writing a post are also easy icebreakers to a high-level connection. Who doesn't want free exposure? That's your digital street cred.

> **Quiver-Tip:** When tagging a person, always enter their last name first to save a ton of time. There are fewer "Galifianakises" than "Zachs."

Documents: What's up with Docs?

The Documents section is one of the most dynamic but underused features on LinkedIn®. Want to know why? Most people don't know about this secret, especially how to rub the genie. It's only a few clicks to dynamic posting.

When I say dynamic, I mean split-second engagement if executed adeptly.

LinkedIn® Document Quiver

- ➢ **Large Documents & Exposure**: "The file size cannot exceed 100MB and 300 pages. The following file types are supported: PPT, PPTX, DOC, DOCX and PDF." Reference LinkedIn® Help.

- ➢ **Search Engine Nullification**: Static documents don't cling to search engines because they are basically a picture. So we have a simple solution. Publishing and interconnectivity to be addressed shortly.

- ➢ **Indigenous or Native Content**: Whazzat? It's content you publish on LinkedIn® that doesn't take users off the platform. Reshares do not count for almost anything except for an *atta boy* or atta *girl*. Don't get me wrong, resharing is a gesture that I highly encourage as a touch mechanism. It's a component of your quiver.

> ➤ Be aware that LinkedIn® often tweaks its algorithm and gives greater weight to a certain content type.

A perfect example of this last arrow is when I reshared Jon's *Tenant's Guide to Rent Relief.* It received 2,069 views, 12 likes, one love and eight comments within a few weeks. That's amazing for a reshare and hands down my personal record. Comparatively, the stats in the previous section speak for themselves at 35,000+ views, 171 likes, 13 hover emojis, 55 comments and a whopping 29 reshares. There's no comparison, except a 5 to 10 percent return on reshares vs. native content.

> If you find a reshare dud, give it a makeover. You may have an engagement bomb.

Infographics Appeal to the Masses

I like them myself and they tell a quick story. If done up with style, charts and diagrams seduce the eye and enhance its ability to see patterns and trends. A clear infographic is worth a thousand words. So take care to craft striking imagery that gives an overview of your topic. Visual appeal leads to vibrant reads.

Word to the wise: Customize. There's a price for customization, but infographics are creators of instant engagement and awareness, and ultimate monetization.

Annotate to Dominate

> "Drawing is a kind of hypnotism: One looks in such a way that he comes and takes a seat on the paper." **–PABLO PICASSO**

Surprise your audience with highlights, comments and markings of what touched you emotionally, written by hand. Typing doesn't have the same impact! A digital stylus functions like an old-school calligraphy pen, reflecting your handwriting and stylistic flair.

Humanized digital touch arrows will touch people viscerally and morph to native content. Hand-annotated articles, presentations, vignettes, case studies and even websites typically receive thundering engagement. So let the digital ink flow and establish a personal connection through the lost art of the hand-scrawled image. Rarity bestows value.

Quiver Examples

ROBERT GREENE ANNOTATIONS

Robert Greene's annotated posts consistently receive solid views and engagement from thinkers and readers:

50th Law Annotated Post

- ➢ Likes: 9
- ➢ Hover: 1
- ➢ Comments: 5
- ➢ Views: 2,022

The Laws of Human Nature Annotated Post

- ➢ Likes: 17
- ➢ Comments: 3
- ➢ Views: 3,456

Marcus Camacho Post (My Mentee—He's a huge fan too!)

- ➢ Likes: 23
- ➢ Hovers: 1
- ➢ Views: 2,301
- ➢ Comments: 5

Ready or not, time to jot down some shoptalk. Go. You'll find plenty of writing tools out there for touch screens. My inner gearhead steered me to Microsoft's Surface Studio as I began scribbling in earnest. What I can tell you about the experience and results is that a Drawboard PDF-enabled note rendered with a Surface pen gives a *Star Wars* feel and is the lightsaber I used to outline, organize and write *Tactical LinkedIn® Secrets*. Another Force-wielder in my responsive design galaxy is touch technology that tracks my work process like an analog whiteboard. The process is called "mind mapping."

The handwritten note is a diminishing art that may be kept alive by scribes, calligraphers and retro-forward-thinking LinkedIn® users.

Mind Map

"A mind map is a diagram used to visually organize information. A mind map is hierarchical and shows relationships among pieces of the whole. It is often created around a single concept, drawn as an image in the center of a blank page, to which associated representations of ideas such as images, words and parts of words are added. Major ideas are connected directly to the central concept, and other ideas branch out from those major ideas. Mind maps can also be drawn by hand, either as 'notes' during a lecture, meeting or planning session, for example, or as higher quality pictures when more time is available. Mind maps are considered to be a type of spider diagram."

–WIKIPEDIA

Time to tier up shortform videos. Not games. What time is it? Game time!

TOPIC 4:

DIGITIZATION FUSED WITH HUMANIZATION

SHOWCASED ACROSS GENERATIONS

Had you told me a few years ago I'd be making short videos talking about social media, I would have quiver-dismissed that comment. No doubt! I never intended to be some sort of camera personality or influencer. I still think that word is quasi-stupid. I was executing on a slew of clandestinely channeled real estate deals and quietly taking small bites of market share.

By design I operated in the shadows. Then realization dawned. Suddenly I saw the relevance of relevance. I started with writing because that's my release. Immediately and reluctantly, I realized the power of short videos. Humans crave interactions with other humans, even if that means hanging out with a screen. Let's short-quiver film!

Do You Know How to Produce a Video?

Don't worry if you don't, I'm a rookie too! Thankfully I have a marketing budget and producing videos in our tech-driven fishbowl only costs a few bucks. Now let's buck conventionality and get producing.

Unsurprisingly, LinkedIn® has the real-time tools for your quiver: LinkedIn® ProFinder.

➤ Select videography and LinkedIn® will filter your preferences, allowing you to find a videographer in your geoQR area.

➤ For shiny toys, check out the Osmo camera and companion equipment.

Digital Quiver

➤ Use smartphones & friends: For the budget conscious, our smartphones are excellent production devices. Tactical reminder: don't worry about over-producing if your content is solid. Authenticity and solid quality-sincerity solidify. Everlastingly outmaneuvering flashy, corny, staged, contrived, fluffy and overproduced videos. Gross.

➤ Advance relationships through authentic videography—a living color impression.

➤ Use SRT* files via YouTube for close captioning. Create a link to the process. Screen recording referencing YouTube.

➤ Inconvenient geography? Zoom calls are here to stay and can be cropped, edited and produced for minimal cost.

➤ Budget up with an Osmo or pull out your Go Pro or other professional camera and mic up with a Shure for quality sound. Once again affordable, hundreds not thousands.

➤ No excuse, get a friend, quiver your toys and *just go*.

*Instructions on creating an SRT file from LinkedIn® the QR Code below:

KEYS TO EXECUTION

The rapidly evolving, tech-driven business landscape is an out-of-sight, out-of-mind, interconnected culture. Be the balladeer of a rock-like work ethic, initiative and hustle. Persistence will create a dominative online transcendence. Across successes.

Become a subject matter expert, create content, post it, attract the views of your competitors and potential clients or recruits. You win.

There's nothing wrong in celebrating your wins, just don't mistake LinkedIn® for a vanity fair. Don't show off or you'll get blown off. Let other users tout your glory. It packs far more power. Plus "they" are talking about you. It's a good thing.

Next up in **Section 6**, you will learn to individualize your brand, tactically track outcomes, leads, people and quantifiable results. You will arm your digital quiver with bombs to prominence, including LinkedIn® targeting tools, such as cross-hair marketing, geofencing, envelope campaigns and methods for unrelentingly barraging your connections—with messages of niche positivity.

INDIVIDUALIZE YOUR BRAND, TRACK OUTCOME, PEOPLE & QUANTIFIABLE RESULTS

"Always in motion is the future."

–Yoda

The other day I was sitting in my office talking about how I need a new pair of nunchucks, then bam, a nunchucks ad pops up when I'm looking at thesaurus.com of all places. Huh? Is Chuck Norris listening to my phone? Is Bruce Lee's ghost haunting me? HUAAA! PWAAA! CHAA! No, that's targeted and retargeted marketing, borderline freaky and here to stay. Stay in your face! Unless you are a contemporary caveman and don't look at screens. Presumably, you've moved out of the Jurassic era and want to explore digital Dagobah.

The Force was with me the day I found my social media Jedi Master, Alex Cervasio. (High praise indeed, considering that I'm a Yoda wannabe since age 6, when I dressed up as the coolest Grand Master of the Jedi Order for Halloween.) Alex's gamesmanship creates touches for desired branding results. More about his backchannelled, yet visually present, initiatives and tactical outcomes below.

Meanwhile, our mission here is to equip you with social media secrets and to prepare you for the process. If you're too busy to author all the content (as has been my case while churning out this book), there's always outsourced talent for sanity and relief.

Additionally, an ever-ballooning suite of digital tools exists to help you reach the audiences you seek, and to quiver their contact details. Whether you farm out the work or undertake it yourself, let's quiver-arm you with targeting features designed to unlock a powerful professional following. Let's enrich your quiver-cache with LinkedIn® ads.

CROSSHAIR TARGETING THROUGH COMPANY & INDIVIDUAL PROFILES

"Targeting is a foundational element of running a successful LinkedIn® advertising campaign—getting your targeting right leads to higher engagement, and ultimately, higher conversion rates. By advertising on LinkedIn®, you are getting your message in front of the right person when they are most engaged. You can reach a professional network nearly 500 million members strong with accurate first-party data, at scale."
–Raymond Hwang & Steve Kearns, co-authors,
Unleashing LinkedIn®'s Targeting Capabilities

inkedIn® has honed and sighted their targeting tools, meaning that marketers can now run campaigns designed for driving engagement, creating brand and PDR awareness and generating leads and email conversions. Meet Campaign Manager, LinkedIn®'s ad platform that we'll dive into below. Whatever your experience with managers, this one may or may not make you work late, but at least you'll get to target professionals based on parameters from industry to job title to company size. According to social media software company SproutSocial, more than two-thirds of B2B marketers have used paid advertising on LinkedIn®.

I take my brand, marketing and budget as seriously as you do. Below are the questions I gave my best archer's squint while nooking my first targeted arrow.

Strategic Questions

Q: I have established relationships. Why do I need target marketing?

A: Established relationships are, by definition, limited to the folks I know. Plus some may leave the field. So I need to expand my scope, yet make it manageable enough to ensure the quality of our interaction.

Today's relationships are forged in the foundry of social marketing. That's because a one-size-fits-all marketing can only go so far, and I need a sales approach that's more focused. Time to craft messages that speak to a more narrowly defined market segment and pierce high-quality leads that can turn into loyal, paying customers.

> Trying to resonate with everyone might not resonate with anyone.

Q: Where do I start?

A: Create a LinkedIn® Company Page (see below) that will clearly differentiate my brand and unique selling propositions as the ultimate advocate for distinct perspectives and needs. Unfortunately, you cannot target market from your personal LinkedIn®. So. A company page is a crucial arrow to take your digital arsenal to the next level.

Q: How much will it cost?

A: Incisive connecting can be accomplished for hundreds of dollars or a mini-fraction of most marketing budgets.

Q: What will be my return on investment?

A: Feedback loops will come from Campaign Manager. Throughout each campaign, quivered marketers will be able to identify ways to boost ROI and crunch the unfolding metrics. Subsequently measuring overall performance.

> **Cobb Rant:** Don't just fire arrows into the sky hoping to hit a duck. Target the digital swans across generations. Currently LinkedIn® skews toward an older generation, though Millennials are rapidly linking on the bandwagon. Everchanging. Growing. Research the LinkedIn® demographic pool and how it affects your business before making the paid advertising plunge.

Paid Advertising–Targeted Quiver
   - ➤ **Sponsored Content** is promotional media that's paid for by a marketer and produced and distributed by another brand, influencer or publisher. Like native ads, which are created and paid for by the advertiser, sponsored content aims to blend in naturally with a forum.

| Native = Engagement

LinkedIn® Sponsored Content comes in single image, carousel image and video formats. Here's why I like it:

- o It gets your content in front of customers you want to reach where they're already engaging with topics that are relevant to your brand. No brainer.
- o Any mention of your brand plays more organically and credibly than an intrusive ad. Plus they are annoying as shiznit.
- o Sponsoring content from a trusted publisher can double a marketer's lift over branded advertising. Tracking and patterns.
- o The cost of a lead from paid LinkedIn® advertising averages about $75, based on a high/low range of $99-$51. Pricier than Facebook and Twitter ads—and not suited to every company's coffers—but a surer way to nab quality leads and well worth the outlay if you can spring for it.

➢ **Direct Sponsored Content** is sponsored media that is shown in the feed of targeted LinkedIn® users but not on your organization's LinkedIn® Page or Showcase Page. It lets you customize, check out and augment the efficacy of your content for a target audience without gumming up your LinkedIn® Page. Like sponsored ads, the formats are single image, carousel image or video. Freelanced content.

➢ **Sponsored InMail**: LinkedIn®'s messenger platform lets you snap your bow and hit prospects in their personal inboxes with compelling calls to action. Caveat: As your first touchpoint with a high-level prospect who may not know you or your company, Sponsored InMail can seem too pushy and invasive. Especially for a tip-of-the-funnel prospect. Directly and sharply. Re-engaging a prospect who has meaningfully interacted with your brand in the past? Or pitching cold to a mid-funnel prospect? Up your chances of eliciting a response by composing CTAs with proven keywords such as: try, register, reserve, join, confirm and download. But nothing too formal that reeks of a sales catalogue.

Cobb Rant: Rather, strike a conversational tone as if you're engaging the person in a discussion, which you are. If done with panache, your open rates stand to dwarf those of similar strategies implemented through regular email campaigns and other social networks. Most of your competition only knows how to self-promote. Exploit.

➢ **Text Ads:** LinkedIn®'s version of Google or Bling search ads lurk in the sidebar and charge you on a pay-per-click or impression basis. They're basically garden-variety text blocks with a headline and company logo. Yawn. Why?

➢ **Programmatic display Ads:** Select your preferred exchange platform and purchase inventory via open or private auctions. Never used till now.

➢ **Dynamic Ads:** LinkedIn® advertising is at its most personalized with this ad type. Help yourself to templates and auto-translation options for tailoring your creative assets.

➢ **LinkedIn® Audience Network:** Want to scale up your targeted audience to include other LinkedIn® users with comparable attributes? If so, you're probably tempted to leave the "Enable Audience Expansion" option on. Resist temptation. The platform's criteria for stretching audience are simply too murky. LinkedIn® might know the hidden data that sort users who match your targeting criteria from those who pack on other characteristics (because of this expansion). But you don't.

Cobb Rant: I call them mirrored relationships. Go after them. These are people with the same objectives, goals and targets. Your goal is to target their targets. Facebook pulled this genie out of the cyberbottle when they created Lookalike Audiences.

"Facebook is the pioneer that corralled and fenced Lookalike Audiences in first place...Other mediums hopped on quickly."
–ARTICLE: *LINKEDIN® GOT LINKEDON TO LOOKALIKE AUDIENCES.*

Overview of LinkedIn® Lookalike Audiences
- o After your campaign wraps, you can assess its success based on the demographic impact reports and start experimenting. Then, wearing your white lab coat, activate the Similar Audiences option and run a separate campaign designed to see what it dredges up. Lookalike audiences can mean loyal followings. Look ahead and grow deep grass roots.

Note that the LinkedIn® Audience Network feature is mostly for campaigns seeking to generate conversions or clicks for sponsored ads. And it doesn't work for campaigns that utilize the Lead Gen Form format or for text and InMail ad types.

> **LinkedIn® Marketing Partners:** No need to go it alone when you can link up with LinkedIn®'s global community of tech and service providers bearing its seal of approval. Partnerships await you in ad technology, media buying and marketing analytics, all cocked and ready to help save precious time and polish your campaign performance.

Now that you've gotten a taste of Campaign Manager, you can start to test, plan and receive beta feedback. Make sure your messages are clear, concise, budgeted and strategically targeted. You will score leads, build lists, continually touch and ultimately produce a holistic marketing strategy with state-of the-art solutions.

LinkedIn® Marketing Solutions

Many LinkedIn® surfers have no idea of the impact LinkedIn® has on B2B growth. LinkedIn® holds more than 30 million company profiles, and in 2019 generated $6.8 billion in revenue. The top three most followed companies are:

The sheer number of interactions makes LinkedIn® a cultivable terrace for relationships. I am going to assume that if you have read this far, the company you work for, manage or own has a LinkedIn® Company Page. If not, it's as easy as signing up for a traditional page at LinkedIn® Pages.

LinkedIn® has over:

> 30 million companies.
> 20 million job openings.
> 90,000 schools.
> 100 million job applications every month.

➤ 41 percent of millionaires use LinkedIn®.

➤ The average CEO has 930 connections.

➤ LinkedIn® Message Ads deliver a 40 percent conversion rate.

➤ How-to and List posts perform the best on LinkedIn®.

➤ 90 million LinkedIn® users are senior-level influencers and 63 million are in decision-making positions.

Simply put, you can't do any targeted marketing without a Company Page. It's a monumental advantage to have one—or a dilemma, depending on your company structure. If you work in the corporate world, you probably have little or no say in your marketing department. People are the new currency online. Not logos. And the budget and time you can throw at flexing your visibility, credibility and engage ability are nano by comparison.

All the more reason to optimize your thought leadership platform so you and your PDR are in front of enough prospects with enough value to grab enough attention from your leads. Impel expertise and repel corporate conventionality. Stand out.

Cobb Rant: Quiver-PDR = PBR. No, not Pabst Blue Ribbon. I used to beer bong in college, but rather personal brand recognition. Up your game to champagne.

Quiver Tactic–Arrows

➤ Shoot #1: Even if you work for a large corporation or organization, create a Company Page, microsite or website for your personal brand (PDR). Digital Autonomy = Power (Callout)

➤ Shoot #2: Create a personally branded logo and microsite or full website.

- o Insert TLS microsite—TacticalLinkedIn®Secrets.com
- o Branded Assets: banner, logo, book cover, email signature.
- o Branded Handles.
- ➤ Shoot #3: Tie your microsite branding to your LinkedIn® Showcase Page. LinkedIn® Showcase Pages are extensions of your LinkedIn® Company Page where you can bolster your brand, business unit or initiative by rallying followers around your content. Let your beacon shine. Highlight positive attributes.
- ➤ Shoot #4: Research campaigns and lace your targets through Sales Navigator.

Create a Showcase Page

TACTICAL APPLICATION #1:
MICROSOFT 365 (SHOWCASE PAGE):

The Showcase Page is a peek behind Willy Wonka's curtain. Especially if used in tandem with Surface Duo, Microsoft's dual-screen mobile device and transcription feature that enables users to record conversations directly to Word and have them transcribed automatically. Prerecorded audio files and videos can also be uploaded and turned into editable and searchable transcription from within Word.

Reality Bites–into Market Share

Let's nibble away market share in real-time, following real-world examples reinforced through real lessons. Real executions below. Success processes don't need to be complicated or cumbersome.

> **Cobb Rant:** Yep, step in threes across the Mongolian steppe. We'll detail the process our publishing team used to implement our own secrets and get this book in front of a diverse battlesphere.

The key? Diversified dynamic marketing assets. Below are your tactical steps for traversing the next level steppe:

Quiver–Dynamic Assets

➢ Create, update or reinvigorate your intellectual property on your Personally Branded Website (PBW) Company or Showcase Page.

➢ Marketing asset checklist
  o Website, microsite or landing site
  o LinkedIn® banner
  o Branded LinkedIn® professional photo
  o Branded signature: Brand your signature with dynamic imagery to differentiate your brand.
  o Branded photo: Showcase a hashtag or website next to your picture for mass promotion.

> Cross-pollinate branded images on a minimum of three mediums.
> Drive traffic to your website and ensnare.

Cobb Rants Re: Cobb Sites

Personally Branded Website: DaveCobb33.com

Designed as a landing/tracking page to showcase various attributes. Versatility. Entrepreneurability. Credibility. Also created for the specific book initiative. Traffic funnel for emails. Marketability. Saleabillty. Repositability. Credibility.

Archon Commercial Website: Archonca.com

Constructed to compete at the highest levels in commercial real estate. CRE agility. Market adaptability. Relevance demonstrability.

Handle Your Shiznit

Make your branding easy to identify. Stay consistent across all platforms. I happen to move in threes, so here's my example:

> LinkedIn® (@davecobb33) https://www.LinkedIn®.com/in/davecobb33/

➢ Twitter (@davecobb33)

➢ Instagram (@davecobb33)

➢ Facebook (@davecobb333). Had to add an extra three because another Dave Cobb likes the number 33. Newman! (You've never seen *Seinfeld*?!)

Consistency, convenience and cross-searchability = cross pollination and fertilization to serious lucratization of attention market share. Just go lucratize.

Corollary: Size & Maneuverability

Building your LinkedIn® tribe starts with building your LinkedIn® campfire. Make it crackle with effective and relevant messaging, tactics and tools that will fire up users and search rankings alike. Make it glow. Optics matter. Frame your headshot against a high-res background banner image that illuminates your company or branding, and emblazon the title stating your company position and field of expertise. It's extra kindling for your followers.

The dynamics for social marketing are dependent on multiple variables. Let's start with the size and structure of your target organizations.

Large Organizations

When I discuss large organizations, some publicly traded, I think of thousands of employees. Among their cadres are marketers looking for outlets. Take advantage of their vast financial and creative resources and tempt them with your offerings. They can potentially invigorate and even fabricate your content. The behemoth pays for your arrows and targets.

Medium-Sized Organizations

Dozens to hundreds of employees. Dynamic or cumbersome organizations (depending on leadership) with layers, but not the complexity or red tape of large organizations. More direct access doesn't always equal power, but strategy and consistency lead to results.

Let's take the example of Bill Kasko's recruiting firm, Frontline Source Group. Pretty much the entire sales force stepped up to the perch for a LinkedIn® geofencing campaign aimed at placing new hires and pulling in the associated commissions to plump Frontline revenues. Geofencing technology lays down a virtual perimeter that triggers an action in mobile devices within. Frontline's high-tech foray into location-based advertising served their goal of reaching specific audiences within specific markets.

LinkedIn® geofencing turns Frontline into the modern version of a headhunter.

Snapping their bows at hefty corporations in three Texan markets, they reaped the benefits of retargeted leads that cropped up ripe for conversion. As Bill noted in my follow-up interview with him, Frontline spiked their baseline click-through rate (CTR), or number of clicks divided by impressions, by 8 percent. The average CTR rate for geofencing campaigns is 0.90.

How did Frontline accomplish these improbable stats? Quick answer = By standardized branding communicated by real people. Period.

Homo sapiens on screens plying consistent written, spoken and visual messaging that signal trustworthiness and professionalism—not a logo or admin posting what might be interpreted as phishing or masquerading as something it's not.

Frontline has a cadre of digital marauders cultivating personal brands that lead to troves of harvestable data, connections and relationships. The life force behind targeted marketed and geofencing campaigns are profiles. Profiles of the people who are recognized as solid professionals and earn others' trust.

> The teams have leadership's support but take on personal branding initiatives. A beautiful dynamic.

Boutique Organizations

Small, nimble and frequently outsourced vendors and partners. These don't have the name recognition or unlimited resources, but are nimble guerrillas in the jungly shadows. Especially if our back is against the digital wall and we are perpetually reaffirming our relevance.

In the wake of the Truist merger, the largest banking consolidation since the Great Recession of 2008, Archon Commercial Advisors designed a proactive campaign to target banks. It sought to capture contact information from decision makers and owners. As I type, we are putting to test a blog as part of this real-time campaign. Dubbed the Truist Campaign, it has targeted friends, Romans and countrymen in the field. Read on.

We knew a confluence of events was occurring, but we didn't have the content to advance our charge as thought leaders. We hired a ghostwriter from LinkedIn® ProFinder who was more like an angel than a ghost. I instructed her to listen to the earnings call with my team and distill it into an article. Drilling down a bit more, I requested that she pay particular attention to our discussion about branch closures and expansions that may represent commercial real estate opportunities.

The campaign was targeted to:

➢ SunTrust Banks executives & real estate team
➢ BB&T executives & real estate team
➢ Commercial real estate executives at 30+ top-tier retailers
➢ 50+ non-competing banks

DIGITAL QUIVER (ADEPT GEO STRIKES)

We've already covered content creation, and now it's time to discuss tactical content infiltration leading to communication and domination! Your new weapon is targeted content campaigns to retarget those who engage. Aim that crosshair. On whom? Any company, person or geographically delineated fence you want. Repetitively striking your message.

Google Earth was born in the 3-D gaming soup, but the only game we're on about here gives content marketers a winning hand through geospatial data. Let's say (in a post-pandemic world), there's a marquee event where the players in your field are expected. Grab your mobile device and fence the building. You're only a few steps away from delivering your custom content to anyone within that airspace.

Here's how: Click on the "+" sign at the top of the Google Earth magnification slider. Type an address and zoom in like a voyeuristic bald eagle, encircle the prey and descend on their screens. Lace the target, identify the time your objective arrives and encompass their devices like a Hunnic horde. Detailed steps to steppe execution forthcoming.

I did something in Las Vegas that I want to stay in Vegas. But what the hay? I'll tell you the story in a bit. (Don't worry to my boys reading this—not talking about my bachelor party.) Ok, Atilla, let's drop bombs and make it a thrilla in Manilla. Strategically and digitally envelope and impress.

Cobb Rant: When I say envelope, I mean encompass. Shadow. Ping their phones. Your magical message can, and will, appear on their device. Mice we are. Lost in a maze of incessant checking. Similar to a great hunt, ensnare, encircle and bombard your desirables with messages and initiatives. Advertising on devices is a prevailing and exploitable vice. Small price. Corral customers.

TOPIC 2:

GEOFENCING & PAID ENVELOPE CAMPAIGNS

"Every winter in peacetime, Genghis would run the Great Hunt, a three-month-long operation in which he would scatter the entire Mongol army along an eighty-mile line in the steppes of Central Asia and what is now Mongolia. A flag in the ground hundreds of miles away marked the hunt's endpoint. The line would advance, driving before it all the animals in its path. Slowly, in an intricately choreographed maneuver, the ends of the line would curve to form a circle, trapping the animals within. (The hunt's endpoint would form the center of the circle.) As the circle tightened, the animals were killed; the most dangerous of them, the tigers, were left till last."
–Robert Greene, *33 Strategies of War*

Cobb Rant: Key life-changing relationships are your tigers, and the digisphere is a great hunting ground. Creative communications are your horses, swords, armors and quills. In today's high-tech times, the pen is mightier than the sword. Let's go earn those marketing stripes, Tony. "They're gr-r-reat" for your personal brand. Especially with the tailwind exposure of a few hundred dollars through LinkedIn® Marketing Solutions.

Create awareness through a paid advertising campaign. It's an auxiliary conduit to an expanded and quivered email list and following.

Cobb: Tell me about your experience with targeted marketing/ geofencing and the impact it's had on Frontline's growth.

Kasko: We attempted to laser focus on three markets, Dallas, Houston and Austin, using LinkedIn® Remarketing for our initial test. Our desire was to focus on the specific geolocation of a remarketing ad campaign to capture visitors who not only met title categories but market geolocations as well. The ability not only to close in the location but also to target potential customers who had been to our website—by title, company and size—allowed us to increase our CTR to almost 12 percent from 4 percent, and our conversion to meeting increased by 50 percent over a six-month period. All due to our focus on location specific.

Cobb: What percentage of your marketing budget is spent on geofencing?

Kasko: 75 percent!

Cobb: Can you detail some tangible results? Revenue, positions, places, any stats?

Kasko: Over a six-month period, we had, PRE-COVID, 15x return on the investment by focusing on geofencing, compared to 2-3x return prior to putting this in place. Our marketing campaigns are now 100 percent focused on geo for all our ad campaigns, not only with LinkedIn® but with any investment in marketing.

Frontline's Company Page boasts almost 25,000 followings. Pretty impressive, considering that the average LinkedIn® Company Page hovers around 2,000 or fewer.

Why Frontline's Company Page Rocks:
- ➢ Well-integrated logo.
- ➢ Posted jobs.
- ➢ Diversified across all posting categories.
- ➢ Great video.

DIGITAL QUIVER
(CAMPAIGN MANAGER)

LinkedIn® Marketing Solutions
Campaign Manager lets you key in your budget, select goals (clicks vs. impressions) and manage your campaign's timeline. It also offers several features to help you reach your advertising goals:
- ➢ Visual reporting that recalibrates and shows only the data that corresponds to your search and filter settings.

> ➤ A granular breakout of the actions resulting from your campaigns, such as clicks, likes, shares, comments and follows.
> ➤ A bead on the demographics of LinkedIn® users who click on your ads. Reporting is available at the account, campaign and creative levels.

DIGITAL QUIVER (OBJECTIVES)

> ➤ Capture your lists.

> ➤ Develop a call to action from click-through to conversion.
> ➤ Lucratize!!!

For this book, LinkedIn® drove traffic to a microsite as the funnel. Establish yours, lead and steer.

TACTICAL APPLICATION:
BECOME THE HOUSE IN VEGAS

CVAS Consulting geofenced the Las Vegas Convention Center at the 2019 ICSC RECON convention. There were around 36,000 attendees at this annual CRE confab swarming with dealmakers, sharks, sycophants, lions and influential decisionmakers. It's the March Madness of retail commercial real estate and all the ballers play to win.

The convention was awesome, but so were the exposure and networking. I had just started to differentiate my brand through writing, and ICSC was my launchpad. I listed the names of every major landlord in the country, every retail company that we represent (to augment goodwill), but also concepts we wanted to present in the future. With my touch arrow targets defined, Alex Cervasio further provisioned my arsenal for relationship retrieval and collection via emails. Immediately following, my following never looked back and has given us quite the model to follow. Our targeted list expanded tactically, rapidly and quantifiably.

> At the trade show of more than 36,000 attendees, 13,000+ engaged with my blog.

Writing, bolstered by targeting geofencing, was the most decisive single-event differentiator I ever experienced in my business career. I am so excited for all of you reading to arm your quiver.

DIGITAL QUIVER (CAMPAIGN INITIATION)
➤ Create new campaign group
➤ Pick your objective:
- o Awareness
- o Consideration
- o Conversions
➤ Choose your format:
- o Video
- o Blog
- o Longform post
➤ Create your audience.
➤ Narrow down by:
- o Geography
- o Industry

- o Position
- o Exclusion areas to keep competition in the dark
- ➢ Set your time horizon and budget.

Examples:
Unleashing LinkedIn®'s Targeting Capabilities

LinkedIn® Advertising 101: Targeting

Cobb Rant-Critique: One LinkedIn® arrow I believe is missing the mark is not allowing individuals who are investing significant time and monetary resources in their homepage to target market to their personal profile. It's where I want to drive traffic. I pay for a featured section and custom graphics. And. In my humble opinion, people follow people. Not company pages or logos. And LinkedIn® needs to get LinkedOn to that train. Company pages have no soul.

Niche Targeting–Initiatives Initiating Initial Introductions

When targeting upward-tiered relationships, there is only one way to do the research—diligently and yourself. That doesn't mean your staff can't handle the laborious legwork, but you, reader, must deep dive, dive deeper and dissect. Your *wakizashi* (脇差), a

Samurai's short sword, is LinkedIn® Sales Navigator. Create sortable and segmentable lists.

A 30,000-square foot eagle-eye view beckons your talons for only a few dollars and a minute. Sales Navigator will sharpen perception of the relational hunting landscape. All predators, whether avian, bow, sniper or ensnarer, must find a direct line to their relational prey.

I want to introduce you to a tactically secret path I often traverse. The Introduction Path function will deliver for your relational blow-them-away quiver.

Cobb Rant: Want to harpoon that whale? Follow the path and soon you'll be shooting cetaceans in a barrel. Get set to negotiate the digital depths and deals. Reach out, plunge into the intro-sea and swim with the big fish.

DIGITAL QUIVER: YOUR PATH TO TACTICAL INTRODUCTIONS

➤ The Introduction Path function in Sales Navigator will show thousands of common connections you have with any of the 722+ million LinkedIn® members worldwide in 200+ countries.

➤ Click and scroll through up to thousands of common people-connects.

➤ Obscure contacts tend to be more interesting. Non-work common bonds intrigue.

➤ Save the connections with connectivity to your relational mark. Then "X" him or her by segmenting and saving your lists. They are your barrels of fish to shoot. Not with bullets. Shoot for knowledge and they will acknowledge your personal brand.

Cobb Rant: Commonalities will assist digital tacticians in circumventing the banalities of a traditional business introduction, more commonly known as the reviled cold call or solicitation. Ick, tastes like licking a cold piece of metal. Been there on a dare. Warm up those hands before the shake. "X" them fish for commonalities. Read on for a true tale involving an alma mater connection, an acquired executor and a new-found interest in Pinterest.

THE DIGITAL GOLD RUSH

EMAILS IN YOUR FUNNEL

M arketers and cold callers have always needed an origin, a base or a list for domination. What's a connector's most valuable asset? Their connections, McFly! It's back to the future with a new 21st-century rolodex of ongoing interactions. Telemarketers need a hook, and their annoying past M.O. no longer cuts it. This is where retargeting and repetition come into play. Your lists are your segmented customers and an ever-appreciating asset that will help you McFly by the competition. Through email harvesting.

> LinkedIn® is your Mongolian horde with exact coordinates. Imagine the tactical advantage G-Khan would have had if every arrow assuredly struck.

Funnel Marketing

You know the difference between drunk people dancing at a wedding and the ancientJapanese kabuki dance? Planning. Thankfully (or in Japanese, *arigatai koto ni* (ありがたいことに), there was no electric slide in feudal Japan. Kabuki is not only planned to the finest minutia, its calibrated and adjusted at each step. Think kabuki calibration when preparing your next funnel marketing campaign. Calibration based on the consumer's decision.

TOPIC 4:

TOUCH CAMPAIGNS ACROSS MEDIUMS

L inkedIn® is a web of interconnectivity spinning amidst other webs and constantly striking whooshes of content. No, I did not just watch the Bruce Lee classic *Fist of Fury*. Those hands chop so fast you can hardly see them. Which brings me to the multiple mediums that I use throughout my day. How about you? Do you know how many mediums you operate on?

Here are the last five times I opened my phone. What did you access?

LinkedIn®—Outlook—Twitter—Text Messages—Facebook—Pinterest and???

My intermittents are YouTube and Pinterest. I check them regularly, but not as often as my key mediums:

➢ LinkedIn®
➢ Facebook
➢ Twitter

➢ Instagram
➢ YouTube

Cobb Rant: It's a beautiful day to be a digital archer. You're perched, armed and ready. At this point you no longer seek. You pick targets for relationship attainment who may also become employees and partners. What or who are the targets and time windows ripe for your mark? Read on.

Targets

Your targets are the treasure chests of emails that are stashed on various interconnected mediums. Such relationship riches have the potential to become a monetized flow of attention and net some serious revenue. How does an archer retrieve an arrow? The same way you'll harness emails—by getting the targets to visit your website.

Your endgame is to capture your connections and capitalize on them through tracking pixels or email signups. The booty you desire in the chests is just a touch arrow away. Leads are looming if you deploy content to multiple mediums through Loomly. Reminder: www.Loomly.com.

Tactical Tactic: Pop Your Following

Simply put. The best way to ensnare emails is a pop-up on your website. It's not rude or intrusive, because whoever responded opted to do so. Don't give anything away without getting an email in exchange.

Cobb Rant: Don't monkey around. Mailchimp will keep you from slipping on a specific banana peel. Losing a warm lead. AKA, not having a pop-up. In today's distracted, ephemeral, and scroll-down society, any additional ask can cause the fish to break your line. Hook them right in their screen face. Pop them and impress with a pop-up.

Imagine LinkedIn® as your blind, perch or launchpad where you aim at mediums (e.g., email) to enlist fellow archers shooting projectiles of pictures, quotes, videos, longform posts and articles. Picture those projectiles as content, all tied to compounded networks of people and emails—your coveted targets of engagement skillfully captured from your attention-share longbow.

> It's not about how much you know, but knowing how to stay perpetually interconnected. And it's not who you know, but who knows the multiple mediums where you are deploying content and engaging.

Organic Test Battles–Advance Slowly, Then Quickly

Deploy arrows into the projectile mediums. Once posted, Loomly splinters to multiple mediums. It instantly mobilizes vast reserves to help you fight your pixelated battle. Your content will quickly rain down on strategic forces bearing highly prized property. Plunder their contacts. Head back to the future with an organic barrage.

Summer of 1219 AD

"After a fierce battle, the Mongols retreated. Jalal ad-Din reported back to his father that the Mongol army was not nearly as fearsome as their reputation."

A Few Months Later

"This time, however, it was different. The Mongols unleashed strange weapons: their arrows were dipped in burning tar, which created smoke screens behind which their lightning-quick horsemen advanced, opening breaches in the lines of the shah's army through which more heavily armed cavalry would advance..." —Robert Greene, The 33 Strategies of War

Genghis Khan was a master of psychological warfare and strategic analysis. Often, he would instigate a test battle and feign retreat while waiting to annihilate his pursuers. Take it from a mighty warrior and massacre preconceived notions as you reinvent, elicit and share lead magnets. Just as my boy G-Khan's arrows dipped in tar had a fiery impact on his opponents, your silk-nooked arrows will vanquish the objects of your quest. Their digital booty, at least.

Cobb Rant: Loosing the arrows in your quiver must be deliberate and timed. You cannot retrieve arrows fired into the dark. They may stick temporarily but are doomed to fall with an echoless thud. They stick when you track. Your nocked arrow (content) and targeted geofencing.

DIGITAL QUIVER (GEO-ENSNARE)

➤ Web #1—Research the specific people you want to geofence via LinkedIn® Sales Navigator. As you lace targets, cluster them in specific lists.

➤ Web #2—Geofencing is your "Great Hunt." Impale the tiger's email. Then retrieve it for your real-world list.

➢ Web #3—List people-targets by position, companies, specific divisions within companies, organizations, groups, congregations, accreditations and affiliations. Their connectedness is the conduit to influencing collective groups.

➢ Web #4—Affix your sights to kings, queens, bishops, knights and rooks. Aim for people who exhibit substance and positivity in their ruminations.

Pop the Test Balloon

If your organic content blows up, chances are your enhanced campaign will resonate too. Once you drop the test balloon, look at the statistics. Grab tactical stats, hacks and quantifiable numbers for future quivers.

Web Beacon

A web beacon (also called web bug, tracking bug, tag, web tag, page tag, tracking pixel, pixel tag, 1×1 GIF, or clear GIF) is a technique used on web pages and email to unobtrusively (usually invisibly) allow checking that a user has accessed some content. Web beacons are typically used by third parties to monitor the activity of users at a website for the purpose of web analytics or page tagging. They can also be used for email tracking. –WIKI

Pay to Play

You honed your content development skills. Now let's raise the curtain on paid campaigns and how website tracking pixels enable you to target your audience repeatedly. You control the flow and can make ongoing adjustments, via content pivots.

Definition of Content Pivot

> "When a content marketer becomes a virtuoso outperformer, they gain the flexibility to experiment with their craft, transforming the traditional follower into a digital theatergoer. Adeptly shifting the campaign based on audience feedback and engagement metrics." –THE DICTIONARY OF COBBISMS

 DIGITAL QUIVER
(THE LAW OF THREES–CAMPAIGNS IN SAN (三) ACTS)

> ➤ Tactical scenario: Roll out three week-long campaigns with three content adjustments. Stage content pivots at the end of week one, two and three.
> ➤ Tactical scenario: Implement three three-week campaigns with a one-week break for content pivots at the beginning, middle and end.

Calibrated Reflection & Feedback Looping

At the end of each campaign segment, dig meticulously into the stats. The number three is the bee's knees for me. In Archon's *Tactical LinkedIn® Secrets* call to action, we created three pieces of content for each of three campaigns delineating three feedback benchmarks. We chose three specific topics so we could determine what resonated and drove email signups. Threefold and multiplying.

Test waters. The numbers show what worked and didn't through a perpetual feedback loop of beta testing. Try different content forms and document which ones lead to email signups or engagement. Be meticulous.

The click-through data and engagement will crystalize as you constantly track pixels. An ever-evolving pool of information is yours to crunch so you can grow your following and brand. This no longer about content. It's about strategically monetizing efforts, through specific organizations and people.

Look at who engaged, who didn't and find a fresh angle for your next round of touch arrows. It's not enough to pay to enhance a blog. Far better to debut new content and showtimes. Or recycle and augment evergreen content with interconnected content, as I did in #3. It's all about the ancillary marketing assets...

Ancillary Marketing Assets—Storytelling to Connect, Influence & Sell

Let's take a little trip down social marketing lane and visit three campaigns I and some fellow trekkers explored, and are still exploring, through the power of stories. We'll recon three tactical articles plus the cross-media efforts unleashed to leverage them for further advantage. Along the way, I'll share my reflections on key takeaways.

Tactical Article #1: "Black Swan Predictions 2021—What's Next & 2020 Outcomes," by Mike Guggenheim & Dave Cobb

Here are the tactics we used to build ancillary marketing assets for Archon Commercial Advisors:

➤ Article Drop (Write a 1,300+ Word Blog as a Followup to 2019 Blog.)
➤ Short Followup Video

> ➢ Total Reads (Organic & Paid)

Tactical Reflection: Most people are scared to put themselves out there, period. Making predictions can seem terrifying, but this stands to be a differentiator for you, even if you're wrong.

The next leg of my strategic content creation journey involved cementing anchored relationships and co-authoring with a ghost-writer.
> ➢ Article Drop#1 (Write a 1,300+ Word Blog)
> ➢ Short Followup Video
> ➢ Total Reads (Organic & Paid)
> ➢ Used as an ancillary marketing asset for *Tactical LinkedIn® Secrets*

Tactical Reflection: In less than a year, I went from blogger to published author. I want people to understand my story, process and goals. Sharing lessons, hardships and insights has been my go-to plan to create positive brand awareness and drive book sales.

Tactical Article #3: "Anatomy of a Monster Deal," by Jay Adams & Dave Cobb
Third, but not unheard, is the saga of a superdeal and the sage who coached me through it.
> ➢ Article Drop#1 (Write a 1,300+ Word Blog.)
> ➢ Short Followup Video
> ➢ Total Reads (227 Deep Reads & 27 Intentional Engagements = 11.8% Total Engagement)

Tactical Reflection & Superconnection

Think about your most impactful professional relationship. The person who returns the most on your invested career time. My CRE mentor is Jay Adams, and he was the first individual I even thought to co-author an article with. The reasoning behind this is coincidentally threefold:

- ➢ Bonding through collaboration.
- ➢ Giving without anticipation of reciprocation.
- ➢ Demonstrating collective expertise and gaining tiered-up validation.

Though Jay launched his company, Structure Development, in 2018, he introduced me to Ed Kobel at DeBartolo Development many moons prior—a career-long superconnection.

CAPTURED EMAILS, YOUR CADENCE & CONSISTENCY

N ow that you've bagged a giant list of emails, what do you do with it?

Quarterly Campaign Initiatives

You guessed it! We're planning three months out. More than a month is long term, and once you hit three months, going further out with evergreen content is a breeze. I would start with one targeted release per week, and follow up with three promoted and tactically scattered retargets over the next three weeks. And release on a minimum of three mediums via Loomly.

DIGITAL QUIVER:
CALENDARS = KEYS TO STRATEGY
➢ Plan out three months.
➢ Segment content into three categories: dynamic, time-sensitive and occasion-oriented

> ➤ Plug in the links to Loomly. Stack and push evergreen to a future date as trends develop.

Hitting your mark comes with preparation, but you know what helps? Visualization. Annotate to dominate on a calendar or plug into Outlook with reminders.

Once you have your calendar logged, your posts will distribute like clockwork. Your creative time (new posts and content) is spent expanding, pushing and stacking your calendar. Watch your productivity go through the roof with this programmatic approach to casting tactically prepared messages, musings, calls to action and more.

Anchor & Capture—Through Your Personally Branded Website

Conventionality. Buck it. Brand. Create. Through your own personally branded website (PBW). Analyze the competition. Are they personally branded and webbed? I highly doubt it. Why? Because they either:

1. Never thought about it.
2. Harbor self-doubt about their wowability.
3. Don't see a value. Blinding blinders.

Web-Up, Gear-Up, Ensnare-Up Webbed Site Tactics

DIGITAL QUIVER:
CLEAN UNITS & YOUR WEBSITE
Three suggested segments for you site. Make sure your tactical content units are clean—text and images.

First, a word about digital hygiene: Keep it clean. Like real candy, too much eye candy can cause bouncing off walls. Sure, lavish your users with rich media and brain juice, but also cleanse palates with blasts of oxygen—pure air and space. Because how can you stand out amidst clutter? Qi is key. May the Life Force be with you. The vitality and ensnaring efficacy of your webbed site depend on it.

➢ Business acumen, leadership and outward knowledge dumps.

➢ Add more. Business units or ventures.

➢ Personal. Your point of view. Authentic and you.

➢ Advocacy. Help someone dammit.

➢ Clean aesthetic. Leave breathing room. Soft and noiseless.

Cobb Rant: Illustrate intangibly. I can't tactically tell you how to brand your website. Make it yours. Be real in your dealings. Connect. Advocate. Do good. Humbly showcase. Your shimmer will shimmer. Create a mark for yourself. It's as unique as a fingerprint—or my basketball nickname: Snowflake. Pure and driven.

KEYS TO EXECUTION

We are pretty near the tip of the arrowed funnel at this point, and if you've read this far, high fives. Relationships will funnel to your quiver. How and why? Your skills are now that of a vlogger, blogger and logger of hours committed to LinkedIn®. Tip of the arrow executives recognize sharpness in intellect and the self-confidence to share knowledge.

You're committing those hours with the ultimate goal of quantification, which equals monetization. With the added bonus of informing and helping your digital colleagues through positive attention marketshare. Tracking campaigns is the only way to pivot your humble knowledge into big dollars. Big data is the future.

"The great mistake is to anticipate the outcome of the engagement; you ought not be thinking of whether it ends in victory or defeat. Let nature take its course, and your tools will strike at the right moment." **–BRUCE LEE**

SUPERCONNECTING

CONTROL THE PUBLIC NARRATIVE WHILE SUPERCONNECTING IN THE SHADOWS

Ninjutsu Relationship Building

In times of peace or turbulence, vigor or virulence, there are only two narratives for consumption—the public story and the real story. Until recently, media fragmentation has led to unmuffled content. You must find your voice to prominence. Don't get locked in an isolation castle with no way to attract, engage and win clients and customers. LinkedIn® is your B2B grappling hook to escape solitude and see profits.

DIGITAL ISOLATIONISM = A COMMUNICATION PRISON

"Since power is a human creation, it is inevitably increased by contact with other people. Instead of falling into the fortress mentality, view the world in the following manner: It is like a vast Versailles, with every room communicating with another. You need to be permeable, able to float in and out of different circles and mix with different types. That kind of mobility and social contact will protect you from plotters, who will be unable to keep secrets from you, and from your enemies, who will be unable to isolate you from your allies. Always on the move, you mix and mingle in the rooms of the palace, never sitting or settling in one place. No hunter can fix his aim on such a swift-moving creature."
–Robert Greene *48 Laws of Power*

Let's quiver-aim and get in the game, execute and deliver. Not with seven new arrows, but with seven magnificent new quivers. Let's quiver-aim for influence. Continue reading. We will provide experts to guide your superconnection tactics and secrets.

Superconnector Quiver–The Coach with the Most: Dwight Bain

Let's start with super career coach Dwight Bain, whom we met in Section 1.

Cobby: Dwight, can you elaborate on why you always advocate LinkedIn® for networking and relationship building?

Dwight: LinkedIn® connects me to professionals I never would have met, and opens the doors for speaking opportunities with new groups in North and South America who would never have found me online.

Cobby: What would be your advice to anyone looking to grow a presence on LinkedIn®?

Dwight: It's a global marketplace and knowing how to use LinkedIn® to connect is essential for your future success in business.

Digital-Dwight Quiver (Bain's Streams of Influence)

All industries intercommunicate to some degree. Start with streams that complement your business ecosystem.

Ripple Effects

Commercial real estate directly relates to finance, to law, to professional sports. Yes, to professional sports. That's because owners need a real estate agent to find arena locations. Surely CRE doesn't connect to the military. But attorneys who negotiate government contracts do. Wait, I've done a real estate deal with the US army, and a military attorney.

How would healthcare relate to Broadway musicals and hospitality? Actors need health insurance and hotels when they travel. Encompassing interconnectedness. And what if a retired Navy SEAL wants to start a speaking career? They may want to call their alma mater. Or a business coach. Inherent interconnectivity inevitably compounding in speed, scale and scope. Tsunami.

To reach leaders who can further your career and add value to your brand or service, connect through the below mediums, sectors and groups:

Business
- ➢ Banking / Financial Services
- ➢ Insurance
- ➢ Healthcare
- ➢ Real Estate
- ➢ Law
- ➢ Transportation
- ➢ Professional Sports
- ➢ Hospitality

Government
- ➢ Military
- ➢ Legislature
- ➢ Courts

- ➤ Social Services
- ➤ TSA/NSA/DEA
- ➤ FAA
- ➤ FDA

Education
- ➤ Preschool
- ➤ Public
- ➤ Private
- ➤ Homeschool
- ➤ Trade

Higher Education
- ➤ Online/Streaming
- ➤ College Professor
- ➤ Adjunct Professor

Religion
- ➤ Houses of Worship
- ➤ Faith based Schools
- ➤ Faith based Hospitals
- ➤ Faith based camps / retreats

Arts
- ➤ Broadway
- ➤ Fine Art
- ➤ Dance
- ➤ Music

So now let's drill down on media:

Traditional:
- ➢ Radio
- ➢ TV
- ➢ Print
- ➢ Outdoor

Digital:
- ➢ Search Engines, e.g., Bing, Microsoft Edge, Google, Yahoo
- ➢ Online news notifications
- ➢ Blogs, articles, opinion editorials
- ➢ Podcasts
- ➢ Vlogs

Social:
- ➢ LinkedIn® (B2B)—Business & career. Knowledge Expanded = LinkedIn®: Intuitive, Insightful & Inherently Educative.
- ➢ Twitter (B2B & B2C)—News & real-time events. Knowledge Condensed = Instant, Imbibeable & Inherent-Virality. Short & sweet highlights.
- ➢ Facebook (B2B & B2C)—Connecting with family & friends. Emotion = Intimate, Interactions Among Inner Circles.
- ➢ Instagram—Current events & video. Desire = Instantaneous, Imagery and Impressions.
- ➢ Snapchat—Ephemeral messaging.

TACTICAL APPLICATION:
DIGITAL-DWIGHT QUIVER (TACTICAL QUESTIONS)
- ➢ Who are the influencers in each stream?

- o They are the voices in cadence. Pinging on each other strategically and interconnectedly. Goal: growth-oriented dynamic posting.
- ➤ Where do I find the influencers?
  - o Deep dive. We already taught that. Hello, McFly.
- ➤ Where do the influencers connect with others within their stream?
  - o Online and offline. Every community is different in terms or size, makeup and geography. Search out the rainmakers, triangulate with the leaders, seek a mentor. Ask.
- ➤ What communication reaches influencers within their stream? Across other streams (conferences/podcast/webcast/direct mail)?
  - o Anything that informs or fixes problems. Niche shiznit is the shiznit.
- ➤ How do you create conversations, add value and become a superconnector yourself?
  - o Think selflessly about connecting. Spend time—outward and bound. Relationships will boomerang inbound.

Human behavior flows from three main sources: desire, emotion and knowledge. **–PLATO**

This book is about combining time efficiencies, niche personal branding tactics, and high-level networking to achieve optimal outcomes. Moving a tier up will require a step up in your social game. It will require a perfect pitch as you go to craft your message or request. Take the field of professional sports, for example:

Tactical Superconnector: Pat Williams

Thanks to hyperconnector Dwight Bain, I got to interview Orlando Magic's co-founder, Pat Williams. No matter that COVID shutdowns were first hitting America—or that the legendary sports manager was extremely busy bringing MLB to Orlando—he still took time out of his busy day to chat with me. Empathic leader that he is, he dispensed compassionate advice and lavished fatherly attention on me. I wrote a reflective blog about the exchange and posted it on my LinkedIn® page, where it touched people and moved many responses.

It had been a while since Pat Williams and I had last crossed ways, even if only remotely. My own father had reached out to Williams on the occasion of my 13th birthday. Imagine my excitement as I tore the wrapping off what I thought was just another annual present to discover a letter from Pat Williams with this opener:

> "Thank you for purchasing three '91-'92 Magic Season tickets."

And my Pops had thrown in an extra ticket so I could take a buddy. Even if Williams hadn't drafted Shaquille O'Neal that summer with the first overall pick in the 1992 NBA draft, that gift was my version of winning the NBA lottery. Amazing present. Amazing memory.

For me, Pat Williams will always be a bright guiding star, but we also share a dimmer shadow. He and my dad are multiple myeloma survivors. This revelation brings me to the second time Williams touched my family. Dad had just had a nasty fall, and I called Dwight for support.

Dwight just happened to be at an event with his dear friend Pat, who took time off from a hectic press conference to learn about Charlie Cobb. He told Pat to "tell Charlie to keep fighting." And he signed a copy of his book *The Mission Is Remission* along with this inscription: "To Charlie—Stay Strong & Courageous." In 2021, the year my own book launched, it will be 10 years of Dad kicking cancer right in the teeth—six years more than the doctors had given him. The former Vietnam vet and Georgia Tech footballer has made good on his mantra: *This old mule still has some kick!*

There's a ripple effect to superconnecting.

DIGITAL QUIVER
SLOW-SLOW-QUICK-SUPERCONNECTOR MOVES

So let's hit rewind and go back to that moment when I wanted to interview Pat Williams. Yes, as a pizza-faced pube, I had gotten a taste of his kindness to strangers. Inherent and perpetual communal advocacy. But now it was nearly three decades later, and I wasn't about to summon up some tweener tale.

Thankfully, LinkedIn® allowed me a strategic introduction. Rather than contact Williams directly, I let my writings on LinkedIn® create the credibility and clout to initiate the connection. The topic? My social marketing advocacy efforts with the Ty Cobb Museum. What finally roped Pat into endorsing this book was a 1-2 combo consisting of a Real Estate Post (Jab) a Vlog Interview (Cross) and a Reflection Article (Uppercut).

The same positive attitude that (together with the wonders of medical science) has helped warriors from Pat Williams to my dad live full and rich lives can also drive your boldest professional moves. A can-do attitude goes a long way when you're figuring out whether and how to reach out to a whale.

Use sensory-rich wording and visuals that make your audience see and hear what you want to say. If your writing is powerful and evocative, they'll even feel, taste and smell it. Visceral. Then relatable. Google "writing power words." Conciseness is the nicest—as your audience will agree.

| Get to the point. Wordy = Fluff.

Think about what's in the reader's best interest. How can you make topics that interest you also interest them? Research touchpoints and commonalities. Mine with Pat were a love of basketball and a loathing of cancer—along with memories of magical presents.

REALITY BITES
–INTO MARKET SHARE–
THROUGH PERSONAL BRANDING

Let's nibble away at marketshare in real-time, following real-world examples reinforced through real lessons.

The key to success? Diversified dynamic marketing assets. Below are your tactical steps for traversing the next-level steppe:

Quiver–Dynamic Assets
- ➢ Create, update or reinvigorate your intellectual property on your Company or Showcase Page.
- ➢ Marketing asset checklist
  - o Website, microsite or landing site.
  - o LinkedIn® banner.
  - o Branded LinkedIn® professional photo.

- o Branded signature: Brand your signature with dynamic imagery to differentiate your brand.
  - o Branded photo: Showcase your hashtag(s), website(s) or YouTube channel URL(s) next to your picture for mass promotion.
- ➤ Cross-pollinate branded images on a minimum of three mediums.
- ➤ Drive traffic to your website and ensnare.
- ➤ Cobb's Triumvirate of Transitivity
  - o Connection Base—Cultivation Across Mediums
  - o Base in Business or Advocacy
  - o Digital Personal Brand Recognition—Leading to Personal Brand Package

Key Reiteration to Execution: Boosting Cross-Platform Branding

Make your branding easy to identify. Stay consistent across all platforms. As you know, I happen to move in threes, so here's my example:

- ➤ LinkedIn® (@davecobb33)
- ➤ https://www.LinkedIn®.com/in/davecobb33/
- ➤ Twitter (@davecobb33)
- ➤ Instagram (@davecobb33)
- ➤ Facebook (@davecobb333). Had to an extra three because another Dave Cobb likes the number 33. He's probably a superfreak.

Cobb Rant: Consistency, convenience and cross-searchability = cross pollination and fertilization to serious lucratization with rewards, profitability and increased marketshare. Maximize all platforms.

Linked Out or LinkedIn® to: Twitter? Facebook? & Instagram?

Another part of niche specialization is not trying to shoot every arrow everywhere. That's when I call my ninja friends... *Help I need your digital Yoda!*

 Digital-Quiver

➢ **Strike Fast & First**—Once a story breaks, so does your virality splash opportunity.

➢ **First to Market + Trend = Viral**—Identify a trend, get ahead of it creatively and your content will go viral. Or find something really hilarious or weird.

➢ **Consistency & Quickness Across Mediums**—You will own your online marketing competition.

Cobb Rant: I learned a lesson about *strike fast and first* the hard way. I had completed a deal with an allied competitor. Indulge me for going oxymoronic here, but compete and collaborate are the constant push me pull you of high-level CRE. But I digress. About that deal.... It was a lucrative one with a national retailer. Great exposure.

But I got lazy. Instead of driving over to the site and snapping a picture, I sent the competing principal an email requesting visuals from the retailer. I even said to post on LinkedIn®. I didn't realize he had hired a young and digitally savvy executor. She beat me to the punch, and my post about the same deal garnered around 25 percent of the engagement. Touché. Strike first or your message will be stale and digested.

Tactical Advocate Superconnection–Rooted in Pastoring & Commercial Real Estate

I first met John Crossman when I was a first-year MBA student at the Crummer Graduate school of business. At age 35, John was already superconnecting with higher education circles and sharing knowledge.

Fast-forward a few fortnights and John is now a writer. His book, *Career Killers/Career Builders,* is a great read for young people. He elicits empathy, along with candor. Like John.

Like all the connectors you've read about in this book, John is a producer and organizer. He manages teams and coaches individuals. In addition to authoring books, he writes shortform articles and executes on commercial real estate deals. More importantly, John had the foresight to jump in early to social marketing, and now he interweaves his relevance into advocacy projects.

Cobb Interview with John Crossman

Cobb: John, what prompted you to get into social media?

Crossman: Around 2008-09, I had two nieces in high school. They asked me, "Uncle John, why are you not on Facebook?" And, embarrassingly, I had to ask, "What is Facebook?" It made sense to me to hire a 23-year-old intern. We took an experiential approach to using social media early on. My target audiences are CEOs and decision makers. LinkedIn® provides a platform for that level of professionalism, resulting in new business.

Cobb: You were one of the pioneers in social media in commercial real estate. Please let our readers know how it has affected your personal and professional brand.

Crossman: My name, John Crossman, and my company, were viewed as the same thing. The focus was early entry on Linke-dIn® in order to showcase commercial real estate and garner new relationships and clients. What we have going for us is content. In addition to serving as a CEO in commercial real estate, I am a speaker. On those stages, and online, I had content I could put out there. I was also willing and able to take risks. I often post an article or message along the lines of suggesting to business leaders what they should consider. Sometimes I get a negative response, but predominately we would blow up positively. My posts regularly go viral. I see social media as a platform for making my extended reach happen. Sometimes I get kooky responses and invite them to call me. They back off. I rarely delete stuff unless it is really harsh.

Cobb: How has social marketing affected your overall business strategies and lines?

Crossman: I sold my main business last year and started two new businesses. My followers on LinkedIn® haven't noticed the change from 70 employees to a few. I can still reach many. Because of my profile and content on LinkedIn®, my personal and professional brands are still as relevant. With COVID-19, conference attendance was limited. LinkedIn® helped me to connect and present regardless of geography. The digital presence is a must. An example is being noticed by a corporation on LinkedIn®, and then hired to train the entire team. It is so helpful in growing business, and it's giving me the purpose and satisfaction of the storytelling I like to do.

Cobb: Can you specifically elaborate on how you have utilized LinkedIn®? And the results of using it?

Crossman: I post on LinkedIn® two to four times a week. I try to be original or unique. A tip is also to share other people's posts that are relevant to your work and give context and affirmation of your purpose and services. I also post on Facebook once every day, and the same with Twitter. I don't use Instagram as much, until I see a bit more impact. Importantly, I don't leverage my posts to someone else. When they show up on social media, that is all me, all the time—to the tune of 150,000+ posts.

Cobb: You are not only a superconnector, but also a coach. What would be your advice to new and existing users?

Crossman: Be visible and be relevant. Know your target audience. My place of impact is with CEOs and business leaders. Be very thoughtful about wording and tagging. That's a main play in how people find me.

Cobb: Ok, now the fun stuff. Please tell us how social marketing and LinkedIn® have impacted your advocacy projects.

Crossman: Social media is my pulpit to garner attention in promoting charities and ideas. My father was a pastor and civil rights leader. He has a bridge named after him due to his ability to serve as bridge builder of communities.

(Google "Reverend Kenneth C. Crossman Bridge.")

I've spent the last 30 years promoting different charities that I am passionate about. They need donations and volunteers. And they often need storytellers. They need people who can help in making business leaders aware of the services they provide. I desire to be generous with my social media and help to promote different charities that need a voice. I am intentional about how I post, and am respectful of the audience. I ensure relevance to business leaders.

Check out John's book *Career Killers/Career Builders: The Book Every Millennial Should Read:*

Tactical Infiltration Through Cross Promotion

John discussed targeting CEOs. What Vegas casinos call whales. Double down at the big boys and girls' table. Let's harpoon and carve some shiznit up. Want to know your target? Whale: Here's my definition:

> In B2B, a whale is a business client that is vastly bigger than your company. A whale far exceeds your normal target, and the splash it has the potential to make in your revenue pool is downright tidal. In B2C, a whale is a customer who buys your priciest product or service and keeps coming back for more. In sales, a white whale (or any whale), is a lead that can flood your company's bottom line. In a good way.

Remember Herman Melville's novel *Moby Dick*? The title character is one slippery white whale who manages to elude its pursuer. Whales are very big, very elusive, and very rare. Go get 'em, but be sure to fish for other prospects as well. Careful not to put all your fish eggs in one basket. Monetize your connective caviar at all tiers.

Target the streams! Whales await! Various sizes. There are three repeating steps to influence whaling:

➢ Deep dive. Then do it again. Then do it again.
➢ Strategically prepare a tactical touch projectile. Shoot something that affects change.
➢ Use a third-party conduit to launch the touch.

Cobb Rant: Superconnection deep dives must go deep. Dig for the give. Delay the ask. Advocacy, and philanthropic connections, are a great way to establish a sincere bond. Whales respond to real kindness. Reel them in through tracking.

TOPIC 3:

LINK & TRACK YOUR RELATIONAL TIGERS WITH BITLY

itly has been my go to weapon in clandestine relationship building. It's the lure, hook and reel to real relationships. With Bitly you can create thousands of links, but I typically focus on 10 to 20 depending on the initiative.

Bitly is a link shortening and management service. Popular on social platforms, it allows for link click tracking. You can create dozens or even thousands of trackable and clickable links. Monitor and monetize for success.

Before we hunt that tiger's toe, we need to quiver-illustrate that:

Application Programming Interface (API) Integration

API is the seamless interfacing of varying applications, technologies and data sources. Technology combined interlaced with personal branding and knowledge sharing will lead to digital empowerment for the next generation of leaders.

To connect with, make sense of and transform your data, there's a computing interface you must use. It's a mouthful to say—Application Programming Interface, called API for short. And you'll want to be on intimate terms with this interface cupid if you're trying to reel in a whale. That's because an API is a software go-between that lets two applications communicate with each other. It's what you need to communicate with a leviathan.

Another reason to love APIs is that they can be tailored to ensure compatibility. APIs are nothing if not discreet. They hide information, which means you can use the interface independently of the implementation. APIs determine the types of calls or requests you make, how you make them, the data formats to use and the conventions to observe.

We talked to one whale in the technology ocean, Microsoft's Director of Corporate Citizenship and Market Development, Raamel Mitchell.

> "Simply put, it's applications talking to each other. Whether it's an automobile, the human body or a small business, the key parts must be interoperable to thrive. Whether custom or industry-wide, API is an integral integration."

API refers to how two or more applications can interact to achieve joint functionality. **Bitly + LinkedIn® + Optional Tailored Mediums** offer a deluge of combinations.

DIGITAL QUIVER (QUIVER-ESSENTIAL PROCESSES)– GETTING STARTED

> Use LinkedIn® ProFinder. One of their major categories is Social Marketing. Thousands of enthusiastic experts are available for interview.
> Utilize a company that can distribute across mediums and applications.
> Discuss social media, CRM, apps and tracking integrations.
> Implement integrations. Automation = time savings.
> Repetitive creation and time allocation lead to message inculcation. Put in reasonable set times, sit back and watch the tentacles expand.
> Single-Quiver as many services as possible in one shop.

Quivered Social Connection: Serendipitous Connection with Pinterest (Tars, Feather, Stick Relationships)

So I decided to go old school like Frank the Tank. I was in the midst of a midlife crisis and needed to go back to college and party... Just kidding, I would have done that in my late 30s, but now, at 42, I'm writing this book and my real thirst is for ideas. Lucky thing my alma mater, The Crummer Graduate School of Business at Rollins College, allows alums to audit courses. Free. That's how I got to the classroom of digital marketing Sensei Tim O'Brien, whose tech teachings were fantastically enlightening.

Also through Crummer I picked up an intern, now a full-time executor and mentee at Archon. Thank you, Marcus Camacho! Only good things happen when you strive to perpetually learn.

Soon after returning to school, I saw something that changed the trajectory of this book. Such is the power of visualized research. Here's how I stumbled on this infinite interest...

A team member at Pinterest gave a terrific interactive presentation on the accessibility, applicability and all-encompassingness (Cobbism) of the platform. So terrific, in fact, that about a third of the way through her presentation, I created a Pinterest account. And the entire room was intrigued. I had a fleeting conversation with the presenter following the class and moved on to my packed day with a newly minted interest in Pinterest as a research tool that I can mind map. I used Pinterest for multiple research points and quotes for this book.

This is not just about perpetual learning, free tuition or Pinterest. Think of the resources at your fingertips from abundant knowledge to actionable tools that will make enrichment a habit. Reconnect and seek new experiences and skills. Reach out to your alma mater. It's how I saw the Pinterest light. The key to success, as high achievers know, is the yearning for new learning and interests

Quivered Digital Media: A Media Alliance Bonded in Chaos (Ron Ruggless)

Earlier, we discussed my business partner, Jon Hellein, sowing the seeds of writing. Let's now talk about arrows, bows, reaps and sows. The target? High-level national media exposure.

Enter Jonny's new superconnection forged through LinkedIn®: Ron Ruggless, senior food editor of *Nation's Restaurant News*. It's a premiere foodie magazine in the United States, and he's a culinary business author offering edible bites of insight for the restaurant and commercial real estate experts to ingest.

Our collective prosperity is fundamentally reliant on the interdependence of bricks, mortar, financing, ancillary retailers and culinary entrepreneurship. Ron is a sage and a fount of insight for an industry that was brought to its knees during a pandemic summer.

Quivered Digital Media–Reciprocal Influencer Targeting
Tactical Networking Post–Tara Tedrow (40 Under 40 Awards):

Not much to be said. This was a baller article with a striking image. Tara is my attorney, friend and common ally. So is Erin Simpson, who works for a local architecture firm. Why wouldn't Erin promote her? Get by with help, but help out your friends too. It's how you create an army of allies in the digital sandbox or theater of competition. Don't be lagging by bragging and looking self-promotional, third-party acknowledgements pack more power.

Quivered Digital Mass Media: (Empathic Connecting)
Tactical Editorial Superconnector: Selflessly Shared High-Level Insight

In today's "fake news" culture, I truly respect journalists who are out to non-slantily inform us—and enhance our business creativity. I follow only those who espouse empathic insights.

The first name that pops to mind is the editor-in-chief at LinkedIn®, Daniel Roth. Roth epitomizes superconnected empathy, the most powerful tool a digital chess player can deploy. Daniel is the king of kings on the LinkedIn® chessboard. Let's quiver-analyze how he interacts, interconnects and illustrates the flattening of the communication spectrum. Direct unparalleled-accessibility.

Quivered Digital Media: Jordyn Dahl's *Big Trends in Small Biz* Newsletter

A beacon in a fog of misguided, misinformed and missing-the-point information is Jordyn Dahl's *Big Trends in Small Biz* newsletter. Finding healthy and ingestible information online is difficult and noise laden. Jordyn's newsletter is timely and contains concise and tangible knowledge. Plus, she ends it with positivity.

Dreams in the Sky, Aim High: Prominent Leaders, Thinkers & Public Figures

Did you know celebrities can get tens thousands of dollars for a retweet? They are barraged with touch arrows daily. That being said, deliberate and empathetic planning can penetrate the force field that deflects banal adorations from reaching their inbox. A little connective strategy and serendipity never hurt either.

I told a friend I wanted to reach for a dream. Robert Greene. My favorite author, hands down. Then my buddy and fellow author, Joe Swinger, listened to him speak on the C-Suite network. Joe reached out via email and Robert responded.

Superconnect Proudly and Publicly

Comments were created for interaction. This is attention marketshare warfare, wherein you rattle that saber and show who you know. More importantly, who knows you.

Below is a great example of our aforementioned ninja friend, Stacey Mooney. Stacey is now at the forefront of organizing and delivering phenomenal virtual and in-person events. She needed a dynamic panel, so she LinkedIn®to her contacts.

Knowing I connect people, she strategically tagged me along with other LinkedIn® influencers (hate that word but applicable) in commercial real estate. Meaning it showed up a notification on my LinkedIn® and in most cases alerts the reader. I personally turn off my push notifications because they get distracting.

And then what happened? They used hands down the most effective way to connect with people. Group text. #everyonecheckstexts. And firmed up the details. I superconnected two important relationships with no immediate reciprocity expected. But. Do it right and it always returns.

A Fly-Superbowl Superconnection

> "It all came down to fourth-and-six, and I knew I had to make the play," Mobley said. "They set up with only three wides, so I knew he was going to try to get the ball to [TE Mark] Chmura. … I just stayed with him, waited for the ball, and then jumped on it." **–JOHN MOBLEY** ON BATTING DOWN BRETT FAVRE'S PASS TO WIN SUPER BOWL XXXII

I participated in an interview with Fly Navarro and Irv Weinberg in the fall of 2020. Irv, a dashingly smooth and prolific muse, passed during the writing of this book. I've never missed someone so much that I knew so briefly. And I think Irv would like this book. As a matter of fact he did. I am grateful to have received his endorsement while he was with us: "Looks great! Very fun…love the Cobb Rants and all the references. It's easy and breezy, like the ultimate guide to Linked-in…excellent man."

Following the interview, I was telling Fly about an idea I was incubating: my non-profit, Rebounding & Writing. I mentioned my friend, confidant and sounding board, 2X Denver Broncos Superbowl champ John Mobley. Fly said:

Fly: "Mobley, is he from around West Palm?"

Cobby: "Yep."

Fly: "Noooo way!!! I played middle school football with John!!! Can you give me his number?"

Check out the video below to learn more about my buddy Johnny Mobley. A former NFL hitman and true gentleman. With a heart that's even bigger than his hits. And his selflessness hits home to a lot of people, especially kids. From the video below you can tell Johnny understands superconnecting. His #1 moment over his Superbowl winning play is the superconnections and Super Bowl connections made with his teammates during a phenomenal career.

Time to superconnect! So I did what any halfway smart social marketing connector would do. I had them reach out via text. And then phone—that's when it's truly personal. They bonded. Months later, when the tides of coronavirus started to recede, John Mobley and Robert "Fly" Navarro reconnected in person after career moves, transitions and decades. And John, an avid fisherman, was excited to discuss Fly's NFL fishing tournaments. Now Johnny's gonna compete! That was a Fly-Superbowl connection baited, sealed and tackled into my quiver.

TOPIC 4:

SUPERCONNECTING AS A SUPERPOWER

W riting this book, combined with my innate and cultivated superconnective skills, has led to a burst of new
connections and relationship upgrades. Throughout
the process I have met and interacted with dynamic creatives,
leaders and personalities such as:

New Connections:
> ➤ Pat Williams (Orlando Magic Founder & Author)
> ➤ Fly Navarro (Elite Offshore Angler & Personality)
> ➤ Irv Weinberg (Novelist & Novel Mentor — Passed During
> Publishing*)
> ➤ Bill Kasko (Frontline Source Group CEO & Real-World
> LinkedIn® Marketing Executor)
> ➤ Raamel Mitchell (Director, Microsoft Corporate Citizen
> and Market Development)
> ➤ Joe Swinger (Author, Writing Coach and Superconnector)
> ➤ Jeffrey Hayzlett (C-Suite Host, Author, Speaker)

➤ Mark Eaton (NBA Hall of Famer, Speaker, Author & Taller-Than-Life Leader—Passed During Publishing**)

*Irv had agreed to be my writing mentor and was already critiquing my work when he passed of natural causes on January 22, 2021, having already accomplished his dream of becoming a published author at age 77. I think he would be proud of my book (I'm getting choked up and the screen is blurry), and gave my daughter a signed manuscript of his passion and dream *First Dog on Earth*.

**I had one amazing call with former NBA All-Star, Mark Eaton. Mark died much too young from a cycling accident on May 28, 2021. A post-NBA illuminative voice was just beginning to amplify and shine, and was dimmed much too early. I'm thankful for the brief connection.

Reconnections:

- ➢ John Mobley (Former NFL Linebacker, 2X Superbowl Champion, Denver Broncos)
- ➢ DePauw University (*Tactical LinkedIn® Secrets* is designated to be featured in an upcoming issue)
- ➢ Crummer Graduate School of Business at Rollins College
- ➢ Steve Nicosia (World Series Championship Catcher, Pittsburgh Pirates '78-'85)
- ➢ Bobby Jackson (3X World Series Champ, Yankees '58, '61, '62)
- ➢ Steve "The Hammer" Hammersly (Childhood Sensei)
- ➢ Ed Kobel (DeBartolo Development)
- ➢ Vince Carter (childhood basketball opponent, advocate for Rebounding & Writing and future NBA Hall of Famer)

Clandestine Connections:

- ➢ A voice online allows for messages to the thousands and masses—repetitively striking snippets en masse. Create a veiled message of positivity cloaked in a vault of small circle enigma. Only your circle of peeps can see through the peep hole.
- ➢ Interweave cloaked positivity daggers aimed at whales. Delineate deciphering targets. They will notice eventually when they come up for air. Oppositely, they also move elusively so you must keep moving if your touch arrows miss the mark.

The final arrow I will provision your quiver with is a peek into my own quiver. I will show you how I deliver relationship upgrades.

Cobb's Katana-Quiver

Archon Commercial Advisors Weekly Articles

The process of writing Archon's weekly articles became streamlined once we found ghostwriters to haunt our competitors, and their realm of influence, like clockwork. Every week these spectral scribes helped us make a social media appearance with content so attention-getting it was almost spooky. With them on the blog beat, I could now cultivate my own authorial spirit. I could put the "boo" back in book.

Writing once per week or even twice per month will impel a perception of differentiation and consistency for minimal $$$. Target, strategize and write about your superconnective targets. Even if externally drafted, the piece will propagate your perspective and insight. Find a tonally sensitive ghostwriter and you'll get your distinctive voice out there as well.

Leadership & Subject Matter Expert Articles

Share knowledge, insight and vulnerability, and real-deal people will gravitate to you if your content smacks of the real deal. Hard. And always err on the side of generosity. Elevate your contacts, allies and targets by featuring them as an expert in a post. By the same token, I recommend crediting co-authors.

> Giving is rewarding, especially to those who have helped your journey. Honor duality. The Yin of a humble scribe and the Yang of a silent mentor. Your voice.

In April of 2020 I knew people felt a crush of negative emotions such as anxiety, claustrophobia and depression due to isolation. Many, including my young teammates and mentees, were struggling to stay productive given the pandemic-induced draconian climate. So I decided to write an article and share my tactical productivity. Writing was my therapy. And this was one of my last short-forms before taking on this book.

> **Cobb Rant:** My ghostwriters gin up my Homerisms, but I always make the article mine including the pink donut factor: Voice resonance. Followers can sniff out a non-participating writer the way I could find Marvin's (DePauw University late-night staple) after a binge of boozing in Greencastle. Perception = Reality. Your Homerisms for your homeys.

Tactical Discussions Podcast

The kings and queens of the chessboard win with their message, whether it's self-promotional or philanthropic. They want to be heard. They want their karma. Reciprocated.

Concise Katanas–Digital Mini Books

Small is beautiful. Don't have time or headspace to write a tome? No problem. Go mini. Small strikes that hit home. A mini book might just be the most potent weapon in your quiver. It's the Lebron James of marketing assets. The ideal combination of speed, power and efficiency. Think mini output for maxi impact.

The publishing rules have changed. Gone are the days when you had to be a Stephen King to come out with a book. The beauty in going after marketshare booty, with mini books, is you don't have to break the bank or surrender creative control to corporate publishing houses. Never. Nor do you have to sweat it out for 300 pages. Time is money, and the barrier to manuscript entry is now porous—thanks to pixelated publishing.

Now that you're persuaded to craft a lean and mean manuscript, here's what you need to know to get started.

DIGITAL QUIVER_
MINIMAL BOOK, MAXIMUM IMPACT

- ➢ Mini books are typically 8,000 to 15,000 words.
- ➢ Start with an idea. Quiver-Outline!
- ➢ Got segmented ideas? Create a multi-part series or anthology.
- ➢ Hire copyright editors to mentor you. It's been awesome for me in ranting this sonnet.

Tactical Perspective

To this point in this section, you have read thousands of words. It's not so difficult.

Quiver-Outline, Quiver-Write, Quiver-Execute.

Your digital presence may dip as your social media goes a little out to sea, but once book authorship is bunged, relevance market-share will gush back like a tsunami of opportunities.

The sharpest arrow in my quiver is this very book that you are reading. Prior to writing it, I took a lot of business prospects out to dinner. It was a starvation diet for my brand. Now I can print out copies of *Tactical LinkedIn® Secrets*, add a personal touch through book signing and gift the books to potential clients and quiver-tiered relationships.

#InstantCredibility. #InstantBranding. #InstantDifferentiation
#Dothesame

Differentiation allows superconnecting delivery of your message to upward channels—superconnector streams—leading to estuaries of tiered-up relationships.

TOPIC 5:

FORWARD CONNECTING FOR MY FOREWORD

DREAMS OF GREENE

As I mentioned earlier, green is my favorite color. And Robert Greene is my favorite author. I may have jumped the gun in reaching out to him and gone too bold too early. Only time will tell, but either way it will be the finish to this book.

DIGITAL QUIVER: SUPERCONNECTIVE SEQUENCES–TIGER ENSNAREMENT

➤ Tiger Web – Introduction Conduit: Joe Swinger via C-Suite Network, where Greene was a speaker. A text-book-timely, warm introduction.
  ○ Commonalities: authorship and love of baseball.
➤ Response: sincere email from Robert Greene wishing me good luck on the book and commentary about baseball.
➤ Tactical Give: shared a blog I wrote about how he changed my life.

> ➤ Response: none
> ➤ Tactical Followup: Joe Swinger via LinkedIn®
> ➤ Response: crickets
> ➤ Dust Off: I then superconnected with Jeff Hayzlett at C-Suite Network and he made a super-reintroduction connection after receiving the "Library Version" of my book. He wrote the following email to Robert Greene (tactically suggested by our team)

Missed Connections & Quivered Horizons

I went after Chuck Norris (Martial Arts Legend & Movie Icon) and he just wasn't accessible. Life isn't a fairytale and I'm just not that good at shooting an Uzi. I am still very thankful to Mr. Norris (what our sensei demanded we call him in person) for helping me learn resilience—especially in failure.

And I failed on my biggest target of this venture. Connecting with Robert Greene, my inspiration. Joe Swinger helped me take a swing for the fences with my favorite author and mentor-from-afar. The bestselling author and master of the book *Mastery* and my favorite scribe to imbibe. I missed with Greene. He responded once, but never again. I am not sure what happened, but who knows what the future holds. Someday, Robert and I may collaborate.

In the wake of first-time publishing, I changed publishers last minute. Harrowing. First-time pitfalls are inevitable. But super-connections can be your lifeline and your climb. Joe Swinger stepped up to the plate again. Connecting me to the most amazing connection in my life—a major publisher.

I printed 20 galley copies and released my 20 strongest tactical touch arrows—a 262-page unfinished book. Customized toward specific individuals and the sharp end of the funnel. I can now target the neddle-tips of the spear. A weapon that is perpetually malleable. As *TLS* sunsets, I will discuss my brightest superconnection. Via FedEx. I overnighted a galley copy to David Hancock, CEO at Morgan James Publishing. In one of our initial conversations, David elaborated that they want their authors to have three things:

1. A completed manuscript. I had a fully designed book.
2. The authors to be coachable. I have an athlete's mentality.
3. To be intimately involved in the marketing. I'm a marketing expert.

Our uncloaked Tactical LinkedIn® Secret is the second version of this book you are currently reading. Black and white. Demonstrative and clandestine. Ranterous and knowledge-teeming. Distributable to masses and internationally. Morgan James Publishing and I will entwine and barrage our followings with positivity and subject matter learning. I started with a blog, then a Library Version, then a Tactical Version and I can only optimistically anticipate where the next ball caroms, future writings and superconnections. Stay tuned...

Undertaking thought leadership, high level marketing and authorship have led me down a beautifully mysterious rabbit hole. With engaging and fascinating targets ahead. A book deal and unfathomable introductions, future versions and opportunities await. Hopefully some of you helped me complete my dream and bought this at a bookstore or maybe even an airport, none of which would have happened without my decision—and deep delve—to write *Tactical LinkedIn® Secrets*. Keep me LinkedIn® when you write your book.

"Study the science of art. Study the art of science. Develop your senses–especially learn how to see. Realize that everything connects to everything to everything else." –LEONARDO DA VINCI

CONCLUDING COBB RANTS AND REMARKS

The Ultimate Strategy–Advocacy

May you live in interesting times, which is perhaps the best that can be said about the epochs and circumstances we are collectively bisecting. We're all sadly learning how to navigate collective heartache in an infected, interdependent world. As I write, there is ongoing psychological carnage in communities that are the most vulnerable. Virulence has gone viral. Globally and locally.

In a time of novel chaos, healthy voices must emerge. Especially on behalf of those with little defense against an invisible pathogen. This book has been released in the predawn transition to a fundamentally evolving and ever-transformed world.

Writing is our bond and more critical now than ever. Positivity counterbalances anxiety. Creativity nurtures civility. Writing sturdies self-possession. Sharing light creates sparks and fans advocacy flames. It did for me and that's why all proceeds from this book will be donated to strategic and quivered non-profit venture— Rebounding and Writing.

Let's Quiver-Niche-Differentiate

I decided to niche down on a specific group by dedicating an organization and my personal time: to young athletes of color. Like those I grew up—and formed a deep bond—with through competitive basketball.

My personal game plan and goals:

➢ Identify and recruit young athletes with a penchant for storytelling.

➢ Deeply burrow a creative spirit through developmental initiatives. Creativity counters complacency, resentment, failure anxiety and lack of self-esteem.

➢ Supperconnect with all webs to a path of advocacy, nocked and aimed at passion and intended results. This happens through dynamic marketing and targeted relationship infiltration. My plan is to target sports leaders, influential community pillars and other raconteurs.

Differentiate by donating all book proceeds to my non-profit *Rebounding & Writing*. Through my book-writing process, I've realized it's not about exposure. It's about sharing knowledge. Recurring themes in this book include writing and connecting across B2B industries, including mine, commercial real estate, calculated advocacy, creating CRE industry-adept queens, LinkedIn® prowess, relational chess, ninja communications strategies, advocacy and developing a personal and professional brand that attracts positive attention. Forward thinking.

You can now do the same in your given industry and advocations (Cobbism)

LinkedIn® panorama and your tactical persona. Armed and quivered, you're an apex predator, the queen of the chessboard. So let's think about forward hunting...

This book was written as an arrow in my overall Katana-Quiver. The catalyst to building a new organization based on sharing, knowledge and advocacy. To all reading this, it would be super if we connect soon.

QUIVER-CONCLUSION

STAY TUNED FOR COBBISMS

'll be back. More books. More blogs. More interviews. And more entertainment, more enlightenment and more of what we need to know and be for one another. #PositivityThroughConnectivity

With my book behind me, I can't help but a feel a happy remorse of what inventive types go through when their project's life ends. I cried a little this morning before Muay Thai Kickboxing with Jose. What to do now? *Just go* back to my day job as a commercial real expert? Shiznit yeah and with a vengeance. But now I'm a creative executor. An author and writer and manager and advocate. I do love it. My tactical business teams are my gems in life competition, and in others' lives. Till the day I die, I'll strive. Never let them down. Especially in times of virulent stormy weather. And. Always. Cut the inner circle diamonds and polish together.

ACKNOWLEDGMENTS

Solitary survival is a romantic myth that Americans love to indulge. Like Dr. Dre when he left *Death Row Records,* the great loners triumph through ingenuity and self-reliance. Myths are imagined. To get to the hunting grounds in my blue ocean, it took an adept team of creatives who honed their LinkedIn® skills as my writing skillset evolved.

The cover of this book lists me and me alone. No literary journey is solo. I had an amazing cast of people who taught, encouraged, pushed and embraced me and sharpened my pen. All the while sharing a tactical knowledge of the surreptitious world of publishing. Which is why I'll be thanking up a storm, starting with...

Sincere thanks to my in-the-trenches writing team. Senior Editor Laura Blum and Copyright Director/Marketing Ninja Kristin Andress scrubbed my over-revved prose, changed the oil and ultimately kept my wordsmithing G-forces from knocking my readers unconscious—until the next race. My additional gratitude goes out to project manager Joe Swinger, who handled the constant chaos of documents and images like a champ. And encouraged me to swing hard. A pillar of organization and a supportive voice throughout the manic process of first-time authorship, bumps, lessons, scars, revelations, trials and tribulations. Read any page of *Tactical LinkedIn® Secrets* and see the metaphors mixing a mile a minute.

I have amassed so many debts in the creation and extension of this book, but one of the earliest is to my friend and master audiobook producer David Wolf of Audivita Studios. Alex Cervasio and Matthew Frank: a humble thank you for creative-infused guidance down rabbit hole, with more deep dives to come.

And now for my favorite metaphor—basketball—the locker room is where the redirect happens and where you win the game. So my stoutest thanks to friends, family and colleagues who contributed their feedback, smarts and love in the preparation, review and dissection of these sections. Discussions with Jon and Janet are the reason I'm successful offline, online and in life. To my girls who are my world—Cadence, Sydney and Kelsey—you are my everything and I love you with everything.

To the endless friends I forced to read my tales and spun yarns for at taverns, meetings and random places, the next round's on me. Finally, a deep thank you to acquaintances, far-flung friends and knowledge-thirsty strangers—my following, future following and readers of *Tactical LinkedIn® Secrets*—who unconditionally read my musings. Every word you imbibed, comment inscribed and piece of feedback described contributed essential arrows to the digital quiver that is *Tactical LinkedIn® Secrets: Rantings From a Superconnector.*

A FLEETING & CHERISHED CONNECTION

There are people and experiences that forge your foundation. Mine were basketball and exposure, as a teen, to mentors of color. I want to tell a story, printed in grayscale, about a group of friends who were formative and formidable forces in my coming up.

It's the end of a reliably sweltering school year in New Smyrna Beach, FL. The 15-year-old zit-laden, prepubescent and maladroit version of myself was no longer on the freshman team where I dominated. I was about to compete against approximately grown men with college football scholarships waiting in the wings. Verbally annihilating, as much of others as of themselves, to say nothing of the physical aggression that preceded their reputation. Though I was nervous and intimidated, the challenge invigorated my aggressiveness. On the court we played by the rules. But off the court all bets were off. That's where I met one of my first black mentors, Twain Hill (pronounced "Ta-Juan").

I matured and put on weight the summer before my sopho-more year. The high-level footballers would do their thing into the early winter and a bit later when football was done. Practice really started. There was one white standout. Me. Twain Hill, Chris Hill, Harold Rouse and Billy Smith joined the team. All would eventu-ally receive college football scholarships.

I was about to take their starting position. Yes, they would zing zingers my way with zeal. It was embarrassing, skin thicken-ing and entertaining. Looking back, I can see that the banter and psychological testing were an essential rite of passage. Ruthless clowning! Ruthless and unrelenting, and actually inspiring my competitive spirit.

Well, the serious competition started and this group of teen-agers wasn't joking around anymore. We were preparing to play against Eagles juggernaut William "Tra" Thomas (Philadelphia Eagles) and Vinsanity (Vince Carter—Showcased showtime earlier in this book and the best dunker in NBA history). They wanted to win, or least not get completely humiliated by Vince. We took pride in our tradecraft and basketball united us and molded who I am today.

First practice where we added bulk, muscle and athleticism: I'm a starter and that pisses off Chris and Harold, whose position I had just pilfered. There I am in the post, and from behind, blam, a probing elbow commandeers my shoulder blade. The next play Harold fouls the shiznit (recurring theme) out of me. I look at Coach Lee, my first, but not last, mentor of color, but all I see is bemused indifference. That a-hole was in on it.

When Twain had a chance to deliver subtle—and sometimes not-so-subtle—knocks, verbal rips were never far behind. Talking shiznit was his preseason mantra. What did I do? I reported him and the whole lot of them for bullying, of course. Kidding, that didn't exist.

I hit them back every day and they retaliated in kind. Pain led to confidence and a chip on my shoulder against my teammates. I felt like an outsider and had a few too many bad practices. And the first game was approaching. Twain, who was always joking, but also highly empathic, pulled me aside and took a serious tone. "Listen man, you're killin' it on the court. You've earned respect. We're teammates now."

I started my first game as a sophomore. Debuted well. Eventually breaking NSB High school's scoring record (which my teammate Ladarius Halton bested shortly after), and my career rebounding record still holds. Rebounding is about toughness and persistence. Of accomplishments as a 6'3" power forward, I'm proudest of my knack for retrieving the ball for my team. We went from adversaries to a brothers-in-arms race to collegiate athletics. They used to show me their bigtime football letters, and I became their cheerleader urging them to take things to the next level of ballin' and domination—leading to an education—and life advancement. We all advanced. It was beautiful.

The season started and they had my back like I was kin. On-court tussles, both internal and with opponents, shaped this quasi-man. We sparred, they were bigger, we bonded. Off-court riffs and rhymes cemented our game into lifelong friendships. There's a reason I can bust *Gin and Juice* and *Nuthin' but a 'G' Thang* on stage from memory. Dre and Snoop are still my favorites to this day.

The team bus was where the shiznit popped off. Early in the season I saw that trips were about rap battles and ripfests. I watched anxiously and in awe as the rap baton was passed. Dawg,

I'm next and ducked back for a minute. Not one of my boys was having that shiznit. One of our favorite Snoop songs.

Chris Hill: Cobbweb, get you're a** up here and flow with the boys.

Twain Hill: Get up here, Corn!

It was the most transitional and welcoming gesture I'd ever experienced. Uncertainty and discomfort shifted to unconditional group acceptance, rhythm and flow. My moves started flowing on the court and in the big yellow studio following the games. Snoop Cobbie Cobb was created and forged. We became cohesive because of my black friends' color blindness, and I will forever cherish those times.

Digital Comic Relief Quiver
Here are a few Twainism's:
- ➢ Twain's goal in life: "Be known as the guy with the whitest teeth."
  - ○ *He always made me laugh.*
- ➢ Twain, who was always joking, but also highly empathic, pulled me aside and took a serious tone. "Listen man, your young butt is killing them and you've earned their respect. We're teammates now."
  - ○ *Support in the trenches I've always treasured.*
- ➢ In the layup line when looking at a giant (6'7") lineman he played football against: "That big ole, gravy-eating clown knows who you are. He's older, but he's intimidated. He can't move, and if you never stop moving, you'll dominate

him. Stare him down, play physical and go slay that wank-ster."

- o *Twain channeled fury and I unleashed it on the giant. But there was a joyful art to cutting him down and the other hulking players I encountered in my career. Lean and nimble trumps large and cumbersome—a recurring theme in this book.*
- ➤ My personal favorite from my boy Twain. "Hey Corn on Da, all you need to is get laid a few times and those zits will vanish, seriously man!"
  - o *That took a while and I don't think it helped.*

Twain Hill passed away from terminal cancer in 2015. He was fearless, caring, mean, sweet and I owe him more than I can ever express. On this medium at least.

Tactically moving forward to stay connected and reconnect with those I cherish.

A Letter to Twain Hill (8-11-20)

Twain,

I wish we could have had one more conversation leaning back in the bleachers, my man, my old homey and brother. As age and reflection have clarified, through a prism of nuances, the punishing embrace and tough acceptance you bestowed on me were priceless gifts that can be only attained through sparring, competition and adversity. The former stoked my fire, and the latter sculpted my philosophy—I now see from hindsight.

Especially since I have never walked the world in the shoes of someone of color. Only in a dream, and I go back to those days of awed abuse, always followed by laughter. Through you and the other alphas, I acquired grit, humor and indomitability—no matter who the opponent. They could never be tougher than you jokesters. Lastly, you taught me inclusiveness. An example I will always try to live up to in my dealings and discuss in a humble narrative.

I want your son(s?)/kids to know that their father was an amazing mentor whose memory I will cherish till the next big game. Rest in peace, my friend. I know that smile is making heaven a little more pearly.

Dave "Corn on Da" Cobb

ABOUT THE AUTHOR

David Cobb is a leader, learner and complex curiosity who loves to communicate and superconnect relationships. He has profited at work and life and advocates and rants for others to realize results. And advance—to new areas of knowledge.

His foray into author space through *Tactical LinkedIn® Secrets* expands his reach across industry verticals. The book is a guide for job seekers and career changers, C-suiters and entrepreneurs, students and mentors, as well as for the employer who needs that specific skill set to make their business thrive. *Tactical LinkedIn® Secrets* arms readers with a digital quiver to broaden strategic relationships, increase capital returns and build credibility.

David is principal and founder at Archon Commercial Advisors, a full-service commercial real estate company that operates on the principles of exemplary experience, integrity and partnership. Through cultivating his "Ninja Network" of influencers and dealmakers, David has access to and is expert at gathering real-time and backchannel information. He leverages this intel as arbitrage to uncover unique and lucrative leasing and development opportunities, and teaches how to do the same. His progressive approach stimulates business expansion and creates wealth for initiative-based circles of confidantes within the commercial real estate ecosystem.

David has also launched two ventures implementing a strategic credibility campaign, Archon Consulting and Rebounding & Writing. Archon Consulting is full-service consulting firm interweaving technology, digital marketing and commercial real estate. The ocean is turquoise. And David will be donating all his book proceeds to R&W, a creativity-based nonprofit identifying and unleashing creative-originative power for kids of color from rough circumstances.

David is an athlete and a scholar. He played college hoops at St. Xavier & DePauw Universities before hanging the kicks to study abroad in Osaka, Japan, at the Kansai Gaidai University, and he interned for the NBA in Tokyo. Once awakening from his early 20s hoop dream, David went back to school and received his MBA from Crummer Graduate School of Business (Rollins College) in Florida. He serves on the Board of the Ty Cobb Museum and is a member of ICSC and other local philanthropic organizations.

David lives in Florida and North Carolina, and, most importantly, has three extraordinary daughters.

CONNECT WITH COBB

Your quiver is armed. Arsenal-ready marketing weapons. Good luck relational hunting and strategically deploying. Always target tigers. Tactically-secretly... Reach out to www. DaveCobb33.com. Let's stay in touch, collaborate and discuss quivered endeavors to come. I'm available 367 days a year (that's not a typo).

A free ebook edition is available with the purchase of this book.

To claim your free ebook edition:

1. Visit MorganJamesBOGO.com
2. Sign your name CLEARLY in the space
3. Complete the form and submit a photo of the entire copyright page
4. You or your friend can download the ebook to your preferred device

Morgan James
BOGO™

A **FREE** ebook edition is available for you or a friend with the purchase of this print book.

CLEARLY SIGN YOUR NAME ABOVE

Instructions to claim your free ebook edition:
1. Visit MorganJamesBOGO.com
2. Sign your name CLEARLY in the space above
3. Complete the form and submit a photo of this entire page
4. You or your friend can download the ebook to your preferred device

Print & Digital Together Forever.

Snap a photo

Free ebook

Read anywhere